MW00985411

BUSH PILOT

IN GOD'S

HANDS

By

Peter Don Donaldson

with Nancee L. Dickson

ISBN 978-1-79-8484296

HOLD ONTO YOUR SEATS!

You'll soar alongside missionary Bush Pilot **DON DONALDSON** in the rugged jungles, treacherous mountains and narrow canyons of Guatemala, dodging attacks by insurgents. Fly along to witness harrowing accidents and daring rescues. His thrilling stories are liberally sprinkled with humor and amazing miracles.

Don founded AGAPE aviation mission, flying with them until guerilla wars threatened him and his family. Safely in Ecuador, he flew in the Amazon jungles with MAF for 5 years before re-joining his mission in Guatemala. After Guatemala's devastating 1976 earthquake, he flew government rescue and supply missions.

Amid all this, he hosted his own TV program, drawing chalk-talk Gospel messages.

You will empathize with him as he honestly shares lessons learned from problems and rejoice with him over a lifetime of God's miraculous interventions.

BUSH PILOT IN GOD'S HANDS

TABLE OF CONTENTS

ACKNOWLEGEMENTS

My heart is full of gratitude for the excellent help and support given to me by my dear wife Chiqui and our daughter Almarie.

Also I want to express gratitude to Nancee Dickson, and also to Dr. Al who remained patient as his wife gave months of her time and energies to this project. He also helped edit for those nasty typos.

And finally what seems, at first glance, a rather unusual sort of thanks—for two medical problems. For Nancee's back surgery which gave her recuperation time to edit. And for my broken arm.

I had a fall here in our village, leaving me with the use of only one arm. A bit handicapped, I jumped right in on this book, after having set it aside in my busy flying, chalk-art, preaching life and letting it sit idle for at least ten years.

Blessings
Richard
Du Daniel

I dedicate this book to
my wife, my children and grandchildren
and also to
the many faithful followers
of this ministry
for so many years

BUSH PILOT IN GOD'S HANDS
by
Peter Don Donaldson

LIFE THREATENING CRASH

My flying ministry definitely didn't begin as I'd envisioned. I should have been repeating that old saying *Life is what happens while you're making plans.*

The dramatic shift in my life plans came while I was single and still living in the USA. I didn't know it then, but *accident* and *incident* have very unique definitions in aviation terminology. Incidents are when you bend metal but no one is hurt. Accidents are when you bend metal and people *are* hurt.

According to those definitions, in all my years of flying I have experienced ONE accident and FIVE incidents. That one tragic accident happened shortly after I had purchased a Cessna 180 for the flying ministry to which God had called me. Life back then was full, doing evangelism with my two brothers, plus raising funds to pay off the Cessna and travel to Latin America to begin my ministry.

The scenario began with our family's Donaldson Brothers Evangelistic Ministry revival meetings being held in a tent in the city of Robinson, Illinois. While in that area for the revival meetings, I decided to fly up to visit some dear friends in the northern part of the state. The two believers were interested in my plans for a flying ministry. They were big supporters of the aviation ministry of JAARS (Jungle Aviation and Radio Service) in Colombia, South America. By flying up to see my friends, I could explain *my* ministry and show them the actual aircraft I'd be flying.

These brothers farmed thousands of acres of choice land. One of the brothers was a pilot and had a grass landing strip on his farm. He described the strip as short, with a barn at one end, a road and fence at the other end. He said the fence was low, so should not be a problem in landing. Well, after all, I was going to be flying in difficult situations in Latin America, so I should be able to manage such a simple landing.

Flying in, I located the strip, saw the barn and the fence. Out of the corner of my eye I also glimpsed some posts that might have indicated electrical lines. However, since my pilot friend hadn't mentioned anything about electrical lines, I made my approach, full flaps. Suddenly, a *wire* loomed right in front of me! Too late to maneuver, the wire caught my wheels. In a split second I was crashing nose-first, the plane flipping over, tearing down the wire, breaking those two poles.

With no shoulder harnesses in early Cessna models, I took the initial impact in my arms. I had been pulling back on the control wheel, with my elbow braced against my seat. The whole force of the impact jammed through my arm, exploding at the weakest point, my forearm. My other hand on the throttle suffered both bones broken at my wrist.

Rebounding from the first impact, my head slammed into the instrument panel, hitting just below my nose. My upper teeth were torn out. My lower jaw was destroyed, broken in seven places. I knew none of this then. I was hanging upside down, unconscious, bleeding. Somehow (pure instinct?) I released my seat belt, falling on my head, damaging my neck.

Now God arranged an entire series of miracles. *First miracle*: About 100 yds down the road, the electric linemen saw the crash. Standing beside their company truck, they were filling out their report that the new electrical was now installed. *Second miracle*: they hadn't yet called for connecting the voltage--5000 volts that would have burned me and the plane to a crisp. *Third miracle*: the workmen saw the accident at the very moment of my approach, watched as I caught the wire and crashed. *Fourth miracle*: They didn't just recoil in horror, think about their potential liability and drive away. They immediately responded, jumping over the fence to pull the wounded--or dead--out of the wreckage. *Fifth miracle*: their type of work required them to be well-trained in First Aid, so they quickly dressed my wounds. *Sixth miracle:* the men had a two-way radio and immediately called emergency, even though they couldn't imagine that I'd live until an ambulance arrived. *Seventh miracle*: They gave *exact* directions to our isolated rural location. *Eighth miracle*: Jolting along a remote farm road, with those good directions, the ambulance arrived quickly. *Nineth miracle*: I was still alive. Later, one EMT told me that he did not expect me to be alive upon reaching the hospital in Fairmount, seventeen miles away.

I was in a coma for a week. Surgeons could not operate on my arm or face. Actually, due to the severity of my condition (I had developed a terrible infection in my body) they *still* did not expect me to survive. I spent two months in intensive care and another four months recuperating from my wounds while undergoing several surgeries.

Finally, though not healed, I could be dismissed from the hospital. My father and mother drove up to Illinois pulling my RV. They were going to drive me back to Texas where they were pastoring. When they picked me up, I had both arms in casts, my face a twisted mess and my jaw firmly wired.

Before leaving Illinois for Texas, I asked my dad to take me to the local airport. There was something I knew I had to do right then, otherwise I knew that I would never fly again. Inside the small airport, I inquired if I could rent an airplane for about twenty minutes, just to take off, fly the pattern and then land. As the pilot buckled me in, he asked, "Man, what happened to you?" I told him I was that pilot who had crashed nearby. Oh yes, he knew all about that. Amazingly, he didn't kick me out of their plane right then and there as a bad risk.

I took off, making the pattern with no problem. But when I started down, I went cold! Fear gripped me as, in my mind, I vividly re-lived grass coming up in my face. Then it was all over--I had landed safely! I thanked the pilot, paid him for the ride and was on my way home to Texas with my parents.

In all these years since, I have never again recalled that instant of the crash. God erased it completely from my memory. He had nudged me to take that short flight, given me courage to face up to my fear in those few seconds. That freed me, when healed, to continue my planned flying ministry.

But back in my RV, the bumps and jolts as my parents drove really ratcheted up the pain. Halfway down to Texas, the pain was getting so bad that around midnight I gave up. I'd had it. I could *not* go on. I was through, finished in every way. My body was badly broken, but so were my finances. I had no insurance for the plane on which I still owed many thousands of dollars. No insurance for hospital, surgeries and doctors. Nothing.

Broken spiritually, physically, financially, I cried. Oh I cried, *Lord, I can't go on!* My mother heard my sobs, came and sat by my side, rubbed my fingers sticking out of the cast, and prayed for her boy. With her loving support, the next day I was able to endure more bumps and pain.

As I began processing it all, I admitted that I had hit rock bottom. Gradually, I sensed that God's response was *Good! Now I can take over your life.* And He did! Even though it would be three tough years of recuperation and four operations on my left arm, He saw me through, teaching me trust and patience along the way. Painful but essential lessons. Well, yes, I still did need God to help me find another plane.

Eventually, I found a farmer in Indiana who had a Cessna 180 in his barn. Covered with dust and bird droppings, it had not been flown in a couple of years. But it was a good price. The Lord had provided. The plane did need a thorough inspection before flying very far. A good friend was a pilot and airplane mechanic with all the necessary licenses. He took the plane, landing it next to his house on the grass strip which he used for his Cessna 170. He gave my 180 a full inspection, proclaiming, "All good. Ready to go."

BACK to BEGINNINGS

I'm often asked, "How did you decide to be a bush pilot in a rugged, mountainous country which a lot of people never even heard of?" Well, you're about to see that God guided me to my decision in stages, some of them quite dramatic.

Right off, y'all need to know that I began life as a Texan. I was raised all over Texas, one of four boys growing up as a Methodist preacher's kids. Back then, in the Methodist church a pastor changed parsonages every three to four years. So I lived in many different towns. I clearly recall the excitement of exploring a new church building, the surrounding neighborhood and making new friends. For us boys it was a thrill to move, to experience change. It was just part of the package of growing up a preacher's kid in Texas. I enjoyed it all.

When I was six years old my dad was the pastor of the First United Methodist Church in Mercedes, Texas. That's about a mile from the border of Mexico, in the area known as The Valley of Texas. While living in Mercedes, I became aware of people with darker skin and black hair. I wondered where they came from. What amazed me most was that they spoke another language. Someone told me it was Spanish. I listened to them talking as they passed by and loved the sound of that language as it rolled off their tongues.

Soon I discovered that I could tune the old family radio into stations coming out of Mexico. There I was, six years old, with no idea where Mexico was, yet I sat there long hours listening to those broadcasts. Of course, I didn't understand a single word being said, but I was captivated by the language. It was beautiful. I thought, *Someday I am going to talk just like that.*

Though I never understood a word, two special radio scenarios stuck with me. I have never forgotten them. About sixty years later, a friend from Mexico gave me the background of those radio sounds which were well known in Mexico. After all those years, I could finally discover what I had heard as a boy.

One program featured a little jingle, a play on words. It was "catchy" and I heard it chanted over and over again. I didn't have the slightest clue as to what they were saying, but I loved the sounds so much that I enjoyed repeating those four words: "Mejora mejor con

Mejoral." In Spanish the word for better is *mejor*. The little jingle was simply saying "Get better, better, with the better aspirin." The name of that aspirin is *Mejóral*. So my catchy phrase was a simple advertisement for a very popular aspirin in Mexico.

The other sounds that captured my ears on the Hispanic radio station were the voices of little boys shouting something. First some men came on talking very fast. Then all of a sudden these little voices shouted at the top of their lungs. Oh, they jabbered! Next came the sound of a swishing like beans being poured into a basket. Then, once again, the boys started shouting and jabbering. I wondered why every phrase ended with the same word, *Pesos*. I picked up that word, anyway.

That whole scenario made sense only many years later when I found it had been a popular program announcing lottery winners. The men swished the numbers around in a big basket, drew one and called out the number. The little boys excitedly yelled the amount of money that was being paid for each win. These boys were known all over Mexico as *gritones* (shouters). They kept repeating *Pesos* since that was the official coinage of Mexico. As you can see, my mind was incredibly impressed with the Spanish language. My desire to learn to talk like that grew stronger through the years.

That was not the end of my contact with these fascinating darker-skinned people. As I was growing up, I didn't think anything of our differences. When we moved to Austin, Texas, where my dad took a church, we lived in the district of mostly *Chicanos* (persons of Mexican heritage). That meant that my younger brother and I went to the same junior high school as Hispanics.

As I began to made friends with some of the Chicano boys, I told them I wanted to learn to speak Spanish and asked them to teach me words. They taught me words alright--they taught me some very bad words. I didn't know what I was saying but, after all, I was just happy to know some words in Spanish. The boys would say, "Repeat this..." and I would repeat the words. Then they would say, "Now go over to that *Chicano* girl, and tell her this." Naively, I would go over and repeat the words. Oh boy! Those girls screamed, hollered, and ran away. The boys were guffawing in the background. I have to confess that, even after I caught on, I thought it was great fun. I was accepted because I would keep doing that.

Many years later I heard those words on the lips of some of the Guatemalan pilots. Sadly, I suppose those same words are universal all over Latin America, as are similar words in every language.

Though unaware of it, I grew up during a period of racial prejudice when nearly everybody around me hated Mexicans. Yet that hate didn't 'rub off' on me and my desire to learn to speak Spanish never faded. The popular saying is *For some reason or another*, but I know God had planted, deep down in my soul, a special interest in these handsome darker-skinned, black-haired people and their language.

Isn't it amazing how the Lord was already preparing a young boy in Texas to serve him and minister in Latin America many years in the future? My love for the Spanish language, my fascination and interest in the Latin American people and their culture remains vibrant decades later.

Truly, that is how God leads us along, step by step, if we're listening and willing to follow. How many times have we been unable to see what lies ahead on the road, unaware of what the Lord was doing in our lives? Yet, as we review our life events, we can see His hand moving and guiding us in so many different ways.

Hopefully, through these stories from my life, you will see that *even a missionary* doesn't always recognize what God is doing at the time. The stories will also highlight some of the marvelously diverse ways our Lord leads. You may even get a glimmer of how God is working right now in your own life. As you read, open your eyes, your ears, and your heart and listen to what He might be saying to you.

DORMS, DREAMS and DESTINY

I was glad to be away from home. Well, mostly I was young and looking forward to some independence at a small junior college. I thought life in a dorm with a bunch of guys would be a kick. When I arrived on the campus of Lon Morris College in Jacksonville, Texas, I was assigned to the athletic dorm, since I was there on a basketball scholarship.

Unfortunately, it didn't take long to drift away from the life that I'd known as a child of a pastor. First I began to skip out on Sunday services. Gradually I began to become lax in other areas of my spiritual walk. I never did get into drinking or smoking, mainly because those were 'out' for athletes. Nonetheless, my lifestyle was not that of a Christian. I was busy enjoying my freedom for the first time.

I also didn't play much basketball that first year. But I did discover the drama department. This little junior college was famous for two things, basketball and drama. They always had a winning basketball team in their junior college league which encompassed Texas, New Mexico and Oklahoma. Lon Morris also had a strong reputation of providing experience in the arts. Many an aspiring actor or actress from Houston and Dallas with dreams of someday making it big in movies or on the stage went to Lon Morris.

Drama grabbed my interest. I found I had skills I could use to paint stage scenery. I liked being around the excitement of staging productions. The repertoire was quite varied--Shakespeare, theatre in the round, one act plays, old-fashioned tent dramas and musicals. Each year's highlights were a major musical and a serious play. In my second year at Lon Morris I auditioned and got the leading role in a big production based on the book A Man Called Peter by Catherine Marshall, wife of the famous pastor, Peter Marshall.

I began to get even more involved in the drama department, leaving the athletic department behind.

Besides being an enjoyable experience for me, drama led me into the broader area of speech which eventually became my major at Asbury, the four-year Christian college where I later transferred. Drama gave me many opportunities to debate and try out my oratory style. I couldn't foresee then how valuable that would be later on as a minister and evangelist.

Actually, at that time I hadn't decided on any particular direction to take in life. I certainly had not considered ministry or Christian service. I kept busy, so I only occasionally and casually wondered what I might do in life. This was just junior college, after all. So I took whatever general courses could be applied to any major, any career. I would decide on a major after my second year, just as I'd think about my spiritual life....well, sometime.

Supposedly Lon Morris was a Christian school. The college was associated with a major denomination but emphasis on religious matters didn't seem to have a high priority. There were some activities for those considering ministry or missions, but I wasn't interested in getting involved in those. I simply enjoyed being away from church and all the 'churchy' things that I was raised with. As a preacher's kid, I had been doing those all my life. Now I was happy to sleep in on Sundays. I wasn't giving much thought to Bible reading or prayer, either. I was just ambling along the easy path.

One day at the library I sat down at my study desk with nothing urgent to do. A bit bored, I ambled over to the magazine rack to see if there might be something interesting to read. My eyes fell on a magazine with a picture of a Navy plane on the cover. I had always been fascinated with airplanes, constantly drawing pictures of different planes. I picked up the magazine, the Naval Aviation News, took it to my study desk and began to read. It was filled with pictures and good articles. A section about air accidents and their causes grabbed my attention. It didn't take long for that magazine and me to become quite attracted to each other. I got all the back issues that the college had and began to read them eagerly. I could hardly wait for the next issue to come out.

The magazine's purpose was to promote naval aviation. It certainly hooked me! I became completely indoctrinated. I began to think seriously about learning to fly. Even more, my mind began to focus on a serious goal--to become a naval aviator. Soon my mind was made up. I imagined the glory of winning my wings! Completely infatuated with everything about naval aviation, my head filled with visions of wearing those golden wings on a handsome white uniform.

With that career in mind, I didn't waste any time in writing to Naval Air Station Dallas, right there in Texas, for more information. They sent me a packet of some of the very latest developments in naval aviation. One item was a brand-new program the Navy had instituted. It was called the NAVCAD program, designed so that a young man could start his aviation training with only two years of college, instead of the former requirement of four years with Bachelor of

Science degree. Wow! Two years of college was all that was required! And here I was, already in my second year! Oh my, this was great! In just a few months I could be ready to go into naval aviation. I didn't have to wait four years. I could join the NAVCAD program NOW!

So I wrote a letter about my intention to join the NAVCAD program. Recruiters responded that, yes, you are a likely candidate. We can expedite this whole process if you would come up to Naval Air Station Dallas about four months before your graduation. If you spend the weekend, we will give you all your physical, mental and psychological tests, all the necessary testing so that when you graduate you can go straight to Pensacola to begin your flight training. I was ecstatic and immediately made an appointment for a weekend at Naval Air Station Dallas.

When the time finally arrived, I took a bus to Dallas and was met by a nice young lieutenant. He welcomed me and took me to where I'd bunk down for the weekend--a guest bed in the officer's quarters, no less! After he got me situated, I began the barrage of examinations. I'd never had such a complete range of physical tests before, plus neurological, psychological and aptitude tests. Other tests had to do with reasoning and perceptive abilities.

I didn't understand some of it, but the man told me, "You don't have to understand, you just have to learn to think." For instance, one test showed four little airplanes in different positions and below that four instrument dials, showing the attitude indicator of the airplanes. You had to select which of the planes was indicated on what instrument. I looked at the display and said, "I don't know that. I've never even *been* in an airplane before. I don't know how an attitude indicator works, so how can I answer these questions?" The officer restated that I didn't need to know airplanes. All I needed to do was just use logic. They were testing my reasoning skills. So I struggled through the whole barrage of tests.

That evening I was exhausted but since I was allowed out on the flight line, I couldn't pass up watching Navy planes flying in, mostly World War II Corsairs. A few jets were also landing, navy blue with big emblems emblazoned on them. I was completely absorbed in seeing these guys up close, landing their planes. They'd taxi up and get out with all their paraphernalia, their helmets and oxygen masks. I was allowed to talk to those pilots! I could even walk out, climb up and look inside some of those planes. I was living in heaven, folks! I was picturing myself there! I was sure this was it! This was going to be my life!

All those tests finished, I went back to school, announcing to my classmates that I was going into the Navy to fly planes off aircraft carriers. They were all impressed, but I especially loved telling my female acquaintances and basking in their adoring responses. Oh, were they thrilled to know someone who was going to be a naval aviator. I became sort of a hot shot on campus. It seemed that everybody was talking about me going into the Navy to be a pilot.

A few weeks later I got a letter from the Navy with good news. It was official. I had passed all the exams, physical, aptitude, neurological, psychological. I had passed them all! The letter continued, congratulating me on taking the first step in becoming a naval aviator. However, they could not officially sign me up for Navy flying until graduation, when I would have validation of the necessary credit hours. After graduation in late May or early June, I was to return to Naval Air Station Dallas to receive my orders to be posted to Pensacola for flight school.

Now I was totally excited! I slept, dreamed and daydreamed flying--scenes of that day when I was flying jets off aircraft carriers. What a life! That was definitely where I was headed. But, groan, I still had to trudge through those last two months of classes before graduation.

About that time, Lon Morris College planned their annual Spiritual Emphasis Week. I liked to joke, "What is their emphasis the *rest* of the year?" Nonetheless, Spiritual Emphasis Week was about to begin. It always featured some invited speaker, but this year promised someone very unique. It just so happened that one of the most famous preachers in the United States at the time was in town preaching a revival at a local church. He was preacher, writer, radio pioneer, definitely one of the great orators of the gospel,

Dr. Donald Gray Barnhouse. He had accepted the college's invitation to give a sermon to the students.

Everybody was required to attend that one morning's chapel service in the auditorium. We even had to check in. Well, it *was* a time-out from classwork, so I checked in. But my mind didn't--it was flying high on its way to my naval career. I was imagining that everyone could see I was headed for big things in this world. I tried to look the part. Elvis Presley was emerging on the scene, with the whole country captivated by his singing and gyrations. So, of course, I copied his style of clothes and even sculpted my hair in ducktails. Like Elvis, I was going to be Big Stuff.

Amid all that daydreaming, Dr. Barnhouse's words began to seep in and stir something in my heart. I felt it, but sternly told myself, *You know what you're doing, where you're going.* I was not going to let *anything* deviate me from a flying career.

At the end of the service, I walked out with my books, headed to class. Dr. Barnhouse was standing at the door talking to the president of the university and several professors. I had no interest in what they were saying. I was just walking out the door, minding my own business. All of a sudden Dr. Barnhouse turned around, grabbed me by the arm and pulled me over close to him. That grey-headed warrior of the gospel pulled me up close to him and said, "Son, why don't you start imitating Jesus Christ instead of the world." Oh my friends, that was sixty years ago and, to this day, I remember his exact words! I will never forget that man. I walked on but I felt myself strangely touched by his words. God had begun to do a work in me.

About a month before school was out, I got a letter from my brother, Bud. I hadn't seen him since I'd left for college. He was a preaching evangelist, attending Asbury Seminary in Kentucky. Now he wrote, "Hey little brother, I am going to be in Shreveport, Louisiana, at a mission conference in a big church. It's only about ninety miles from you. Why don't you get in a car and come over to spend a weekend with me? I haven't seen you for two years."

It would be great to see my brother. And I had a lot I wanted to tell him, especially about my exciting Navy career. So I borrowed my roommate's car and drove to Shreveport, to where my brother was staying with five other seminarians from Asbury. They'd come for this missions conference and all were really on fire for missions, for winning souls! They had only one vision and that was to win the world for Christ. Oh, how they went on and on about their vision!

I joined that bunch and they were happy to hear what was going on at college. But every time I tried to tell them about going into the Navy, they didn't seem the least interested. They certainly weren't impressed that I was going to be a Navy pilot and just kept saying, "Let's pray. Let's pray about it." Well, they obviously didn't understand that my plans were already made. Within a month I was going to be in Pensacola, flying. Now I just trailed along with them to the mission conference sessions with a lot of good missionary talks. Nothing seemed at all relevant to my newly chosen career. Yet, unbeknownst to me, God continued dealing with my heart the whole time.

Sunday morning was the last service. I planned to leave right after church to drive back to college. I sat at the back of the church, thinking that I might have to slip out if things dragged on too long. Already it looked as if it might be one of those longish services where the Lord showed up in power. Sure enough, even before the preaching started, the Holy Spirit began to move.

Bro Calvin Vass was preaching that morning. I'll never forget, as he stood up to preach, God's anointing fell upon that man. He couldn't say a word. He began to cry. When I looked up, he was down on his knees by one side of the pulpit, crying out to God in tears. The next thing I knew he was lying prostrate on the floor next to the pulpit, calling out, "Oh God, oh God." Well friends, I had never seen anything like that in my life.

Then God's spirit came on me, too. I got out of my seat in the back of that big church and ran down the aisle as fast as I could. I fell on the altar and gave my life to the Lord for missions. I surrendered it all to God at that Sunday morning service. "I'll go where you want me to go; I'll be what you want me to be." My dreams, my friends, my life, the Navy, flying, naval aviation--I laid it all on the altar. All I had wanted to do, my very destiny, I laid it all on the altar and said, "Lord, it's yours, it's yours."

By then the altar was completely surrounded by people from the church. It was perhaps one of the greatest missionary conference ever. Untold numbers of missionaries were called from that service. Certainly the Lord had touched *me* mightily. Looking back, God had been preparing my heart, from the incident with Dr. Barnhouse at Lon Morris, to the conversations of my brother's friends, to this Spirit-filled mission conference.

I went back to Lon Morris College ecstatic. With only about three weeks to go until graduation, I wrote a letter to Naval Air Station Dallas: "I'm sorry but I've had a change of plans, I will not be there in June to sign on the dotted line." No, I would not be signing my life away to Navy aviation. My destiny had been re-directed.

Well, that was sixty years ago! As you continue to read, you will see that, although I laid my dreams to fly in the Navy on that altar, God already had plans to use those dreams. He gave me the next forty-nine years to fly for Him.

Do you realize that if I had gone into Navy aviation, I would have been flying off aircraft carriers to bomb North Vietnam? Senator John McCain and I were the same age. He went into naval aviation the same year that I would have. Some of those men spent seven long years in prison camps. Several never came back.

I graduated from Lon Morris College that summer, saying sad goodbyes to all my special drama friends. I took off for Wilmore, Kentucky, where I would attend Asbury College to finish my education and missionary training. That summer I spent doing evangelistic meetings with my brother. He did the preaching and I was the song leader and chalk artist. So already God was using those years of singing in musicals and painting stage scenery as preparation for missions.

That fall I arrived at Asbury College (now University) to begin my last two years of higher education. Transferring from a junior college to a four year college, I wondered what changes and new adventures awaited me.

My brother was just across the street studying at Asbury Seminary. I would soon be closely associated with that institution. One of the seminary professors and several young students, including my brother, formed a missionary society called Global Harvesters Foundation, Inc. Its purpose was two-fold: First, to be a sending agency for missionaries. Secondly it would plan short missionary trips overseas for students, pastors and layman. The short trips would give those interested in missions the opportunity to experience in real-time what being a missionary involves.

BOUND for BAHAMAS

Meanwhile, my brother had made contacts with some churches in Nassau. He informed me of an invitation from a Bahamian pastor to visit one of the outer islands where he had a church. My brother asked if I would go to the island and look over the situation, to scope out possibilities for a future group trip to the ministry there. Fortunately, I was able to go. That experience was to produce a definite change in my life, as God used it to solidify my calling.

The only means of transportation to the Bahamas was by air or by boat. Due to the shortness of time, my brother scheduled me to fly. The pastor would be there to meet me. As my brother drove me to the airport, he gave me some final words of advice, "Be careful with the taxi drivers, they will try to overcharge you. Have a good trip." I boarded the amphibious aircraft, one of the old World War II flying boats, the famous Catalina PBY. We took off on land and landed in the ocean, taxied up as close as we could to the beach where a man in a little dingy rowed out to get me. I grabbed my suitcase, climbed down the rope ladder, boarded the little boat and we rowed to the beach.

Immediately I noticed the unexpected setting-- no buildings. All I could see was a beach full of coconut palms stretching into the distance. Where were all those overcharging taxis? There weren't any cars, not even roads! Shortly, Bro MacAfee arrived on his bicycle. In his beautiful Pigeon English, he told me to sit behind him on the bike, my suitcase under my arm. Away we went along a bumpy dirt path, finally coming to a little church.

Inside, a nice noon meal had been prepared for me. I enjoyed fellowship with a few of the believers around the table. The rest of the afternoon I remained at the church resting and getting ready for the service. That night people began arriving. With no electricity on the island, good old-fashioned Coleman lanterns provided the light. The church was packed. We had a beautiful service with much joyous singing and spirit.

Now it was time to find out where I was going to spend the night. Bro McAfee took me down a short distance to the tiny house of Widow Rogers. It housed her and her five children and would now squeeze in Pastor MacAfee and myself.

We walked in through a door covered with just a plastic sheet. A supper table and a single bed was all that I saw. Evidently the kitchen was out back and maybe some other rooms. This was the best room in the house. Widow Rogers had two teenage daughters and three little boys. I never did know where they all slept. The only bed I saw was right there by the table on which she served us supper--rice and fresh conch, a large snail very popular in the Bahamas. Delicious.

Then came time to go to bed. But all the family was standing there watching every move I made. They were fascinated by having this strange white visitor in their home. I was standing there, too, wondering *what next?* At that moment Bro McAfee announced, "It's time to go to bed." So he proceeded to take off his shirt, handing it to Widow Rogers who put it on a hanger which she hung on a nail. McAfee then took off his pants, following the same process.

There I stood, fully dressed with everybody watching me carefully. Nervously I took off my shirt and handed it to Widow Rogers who hung it up. Then my pants, also hung up. I certainly was not accustomed to getting undressed in front of a bunch of people, especially teenage girls. But there I was in my underwear.

Bro MacAfee jumped into bed, looked at me, patted the other side and said, "Now you sleep here." No sheets, too warm for that, just the two of us in that small bed, my head beside his feet, his feet by my head. What a sight we must have been--he so very black and I so very white! I will never forget that night!

What happened next was the most important moment in my life at that time. I got out of bed about 3:00am, walked out the front door and about twenty steps away to the beach. It was a beautiful night, not an electric lightbulb in a hundred miles. The waves were gently lapping at the shore. Oh my, the stars! Millions and millions of stars. A soft breeze was rustling the coconut trees, oh so gently. Looking up to the heavens, I said, "Lord, this the life for me. This what I desire!" And, bless His Holy Name, that is exactly what He has given me. For sixty years I have been faithful to that heavenly vision, through His spirit and power.

Back home, Global Harvesters leaders organized a team to return to that island and meet again in Bro. MacAfee's church. We decided to go by boat this time. A local fishing boat was contracted to take us over. It had no motor, no electricity, no lights, just a mast with a sail over a big wooden box filled with dirt. The crew of three had tried to clean out the part where they stored the fish, since that was where we eleven passengers were to sleep.

We set sail but ran into a storm that cracked the main mast, so back we went for repairs. There went one day of our trip. Getting a late start meant part of this crossing would be at night. I was to sleep on boards just below the deck. With only about 18 inches clearance, I could barely turn over. During the night another storm blew in upon us. The helmsman, standing with a rope connected to the rudder for steering, had a large compass between his legs with one little candle next to it so he could see the heading. Suddenly a huge wave swept over the boat, dousing us all, putting out the candle and washing away the compass.

It was no surprise that in the morning they discovered we were lost. One of the crew climbed the main mast to try to spot some sign of land. Nothing but ocean, which, to make matters even worse, was now smooth as glass. The wind had died completely. We were not about to go anywhere.

So our group leader gathered all of us to a prayer meeting. We earnestly sought the Lord, imploring Him for wind to rescue us. It wasn't long before a stiff breeze arose. As a bonus, the compass was found where it had washed below deck! We were again on our way to the island. What was supposed to be a trip of ten hours turned out to be two days.

On arrival, we were all bedded down on the floor of the church—eleven of us were a few too many of us for Widow Rogers' tiny house! But God granted us a marvelous time with those people, with joyful church meetings. The next two years I made two more trips to the Bahamas, my early introductions to foreign missions. I loved it all.

CRUSADE CAUTIONS

My Latin Armerica flying missions were still in the future. Meanwhile, I will be forever thankful for my years in evangelistic work with my brother Bud. He took me under his wings. I was his song leader and chalk artist during those years traveling on the sawdust trail, as we used to call it. He taught me so much as we ministered in churches, tent meetings, camp meetings, area-wide crusades.

The most crucial lesson was the one Bud taught me right from the beginning. Among the many potential pitfalls of ministry, the most dangerous one is regarding the opposite sex. Yes, I am sorry to say, many a preacher has ruined his ministry and life because of the opposite sex. My brother was married, but I was single. I was so innocent, I had no idea what this world was about, but I soon learned. If it hadn't been for Bud I could never have navigated through that first temptation. I had suddenly been put on a pedestal, out in front as an evangelist, where it is so easy for people to be attracted to you, appearing in *their eyes* as someone important.

Beginning our work together, Bud and I were invited to go to the most rugged, rural part of southern Indiana, way back in the hills, an area known as 'The Devil's Backbone'. What a great name for a place to hold revival meetings! Wonderful country folks populated the farms around this small town. Yes, small--one general store, a gasoline station and one street light. Some empty, ramshackle buildings indicated this had once been a more prosperous place. But in my mind, with no McDonalds or Dairy Queen, we were as far from the civilized world as we could be.

To top it all off, an old abandoned store had been chosen for the revival meeting location. The long, narrow store had been built way back in the 19th century with a creaky porch across the front and big glass storefront-type windows. Inside, the organizers had lined up a hodgepodge of chairs, built a little platform in front with a pulpit and piano. A small group of believers had planned for a two week revival, hoping to establish a church in that area.

The upstairs of this old store building had originally been a storage room. The group had worked to clean it up and convert it into a place for Bud and me to stay. They did their best--two beds, two orange crates, one light dangling from the ceiling. Out back was a bathroom and, fortunately, one upstairs for us. Quite spartan, but it was the best they could provide. We were comfortable, though at night looking out at the rest of that vacant storeroom was more than a bit spooky. We put our suitcases on the floor and settled in for the two weeks. Our meetings in the storefront church began well.

Now commenced Bud's official *Little Brother Caution Course*. Triggering the lessons was a young lady in that congregation who really took a fancy to me. She hung around me all the time, flirting. I assumed it was because there were not many eligible males around for flirting. With no clue that she was getting too forward with me, I just enjoyed her company.

Toward the last days of our two week mission, my brother Bud took me aside and told me that he had been invited to attend Billy Graham's World Congress on Evangelism in Berlin, Germany. That 1966 event was the first that the Billy Graham Association had planned. Bud was to go as an evangelist. His next words astounded me. "Little Brother," he said, "I have to go to Berlin. You'll have to finish this meeting yourself." I was stunned. I didn't want to stay alone in the middle of nowhere, in that old abandoned building, while he went flying off in a jet to exciting meetings in Germany.

"You can´t do this to me!" I was so mad, to think that my own brother would do this. Besides loathing the location, I worried that I didn't have enough experience preaching. Sure, I knew how to lead singing and do chalk art in evangelistic meetings, but I had always left the preaching to Bud. I was terribly upset with him, but I didn't know what I could to do.

As departure day neared, he said "Little Brother, you will have to drive me to Indianapolis, about 2 ½ hours away, so I can catch my flight to New York City, then on to Berlin." Yeah sure, leaving me behind! Very begrudgingly I replied, "Oh alright, I'll drive you to Indianapolis."

Soon my mind began to plan for some fun for myself. So I said to that flirty girl, "Would you like to go with me to take my brother to Indianapolis?" She jumped at that opportunity. "Just the two of us together driving all the way back?" I saw no harm in having someone to chat with and make the drive back less tedious. Well, that wasn't what *she* was thinking. It was exactly the sort of situation she'd been waiting for! She was thrilled to bits!

Well, I thought, this long drive wasn't going to be quite such a drag, after all. I'd have some company, relax a bit. I told my brother, "That girl is going to ride with us." Boy, did Bud hit the ceiling! "No way! No way, Jose! You're not taking that girl one step!"

My response was understandable for someone in their twenties who had been living independently in college. "Well, who do you think *you* are to tell *me* what to do?" Oh, did that start a big, big argument! Angry, all I could think about was my brother laying down the law, bossing me around with "You will NOT do these sorts of things." I had no idea what he was trying to tell me. I had no idea that just the potential of rumors could be a danger to ministry. However, we did go to the airport without that flirty girl.

Bud and I drove the two hours to Indianapolis without a word. I was still furious. I was not going to speak to my brother *ever again*. We pulled up in front of the terminal. Bud got out, turned, took his suitcase from the back seat, shut the door, looked in through the window and said "Well, Little Brother, the Lord bless you in those meetings. Just be careful about that girl. Watch out." I was getting madder by the minute. I didn't even say goodbye, never wished him well, nor said 'God bless you'. NOTHING! I just sat there pouting like a little kid, not looking at him. After he walked inside, I put the pedal to the metal and took off, burning rubber.

I drove back that long road, to that crummy old town, walked up those creaky stairs into that dusty attic. I felt so alone in that big vacant room, just me, a desk, my bed and one little light bulb hanging down from the ceiling. I shouted aloud to the empty room, *What am I doing here? This is terrible. I don't want to be here. I don't want anything to do with this place.*

Well, I had to preach that night, anyway. After dressing, I went down to the makeshift church, but my heart wasn't in it. I'm sure I looked like one dejected preacher. I didn't enjoy the service but I did preach. Oh, the sermon was terrible, the most boring one you ever heard. The Spirit was not there, so the service was dead. *Oh, if I could just get out of here, run away!* But I couldn't. I had to finish out those meetings.

I went back to the room incredibly discouraged, miserable. I can tell you that when you preach a message and it bombs, it's about the worst feeling in the world. I tried to sleep but I couldn't. As I lay there tossing on that bed, frightening thoughts began to form in my mind. *What if your brother should crash and be killed? What if something would happen to your brother and you never said goodbye?*

Oh, was I under great conviction! That bed seemed like a fire burning all around me. I finally got up about three o'clock in the morning, got dressed and went downstairs to the old platform, amid the empty pews and chairs in that smelly, moldy building, in that old store-front church on a dark street in Southern Indiana. There in the darkness of the night, I didn't turn on the lights. I just knelt at that little altar and cried, moaning, "Oh God forgive me!" I wept and cried out to my Lord the rest of that night.

When the sun came up, I dressed and immediately headed for Bedford, the nearest town. I found a telegraph office and requested a telegram be sent to Bud Donaldson via the office of American Airlines, La Guardia Airport in New York City. Bud would get it before he flew out later that day. All the telegram said was, "Bud, forgive me, your brother Don."

I walked back out of that telegraph office feeling as if a thousand pounds had been lifted off my shoulders. I felt so cleansed and lifted up. I drove back to the ramshackle store-front, took those same creaky stairs to that big, dusty storeroom where, all by myself, I praised the Lord and worshipped. I felt so relieved in my soul. But then I began to tremble at the thought of having to preach that night. I had no sermon ideas and I knew I couldn't preach like Bud in a thousand years. Worse, after that mess that I had made the night before, nobody would come to tonight's meeting. That empty hall would stay empty. Nobody wanted to listen to me again. I felt terrible but I dressed and went down. As I stood there, lo and behold, believe it or not, a good-sized crowd began to gather, just as though I hadn't done such a miserable job preaching.

My friends, the Lord came and moved mightily on that night's service. Revival broke out, I mean broke out like you've maybe not seen in years. The altar was lined with people, crying for repentance, confessing sin, making it right with God. Yes, the Spirit brought revival! What a night. We never stopped--nine, ten, eleven o'clock, with people singing, shouting, rejoicing. Even after the service was over the people didn't go home. They were walking around outside on the street. I could see and hear them under that one street light, Bibles in their hands, praising God at the top of their voices until midnight. The next night, the same thing and the next night, the same thing. It was a truly great revival right in the middle of The Devil's Backbone.

On Sunday afternoon about twenty-five people wanted to be baptized. We all walked down to the river at the edge of town. Uh oh, they expected me to baptize them. I had never baptized anyone by immersion, didn't know the proper procedure. I had never even *seen* this method done before. We gathered a large crowd along that river bank, people still shouting and singing. It was marvelous. I waded out into the water, trying to calculate when it was deep enough. The first person waded out to me. I just said, "Hold your nose," then down under the water! I pronounced "I baptize you in the name of the Father (glug glug, gulp) and the Son (glug, glug) and the Holy Spirit." I almost drowned my first convert! It dawned on me that I'd better bless them *before* I put them underwater! Thus we did not lose a single one!

Well, in that lonely time after Bud left, I had learned some mighty essential lessons, in addition to how to baptize without drowning. Like most of our lessons, many were learned the hard way: obedience to one's leader (Bud), the painful process of forgiveness, God's love for a repentant angry man, the Spirit filling a non-preacher, God's power to raise up a new church in a ramshackle building and the crucial Caution Course about the opposite sex.

When Bud returned from Germany, I could hardly wait to tell him about all the Lord had done. I was bubbling over, animated. Finally I inquired, "By the way, Bud, aren't you thankful that I came to my senses and sent you that telegram?" His answer was, "What telegram?"

PROVIDENTIAL PROVISIONS

God was leading me to Latin America. But where? For a lot of Norte Americanos, Latin America is just 'that big land south of here.' They often don't even know that Latin America is comprised of many different countries. Even if they do, they probably don't know their names or locations. My problem was that I *did* know about all those countries. After my upcoming graduation from Lon Morris, I planned to head to one of those Hispanic countries for an extended time to learn to speak Spanish. But where?

My brother Bud had just returned from a trip to Latin America. One contact he made sounded quite interesting. Bud said this man was a dynamic preacher and also ran a school to provide secondary Christian education to the youth of Guatemala. Bud thought I should look into this ministry. He gave me an address for a Virgil Zapata in Guatemala City.

I wrote Mr Zapata, explaining that I was soon to graduate and wanted to take the following year off between college and seminary to learn Spanish. I would would be willing to do whatever work I could at the school. If there was a need, would he please let me know the logistics, such as when to come, where to stay, what I should bring and what I should consider as adequate financial support.

I received a quick response from Virgil, enthusiastically affirming my plans. The Evangelical Schools of Latin America operated with full authority from the Education Department of Guatemala. The mission consisted of three men, Virgil Zapata, Stuart Bundy and Bill Cook, plus five single missionary ladies. Except for Virgil's wife, Beatrice, all involved in the mission were graduates from Bob Jones University. Beatrice was a graduate of Asbury College, as I would be by the time I arrived. Seemed like a nice blending of Bob Jones and Asbury. His letter went on to explain what my responsibilities would be, exact date of arrival, plus other pertinent information. He thought interacting with students would be ideal for learning Spanish fairly quickly.

With my destination decided, other plans needed to take shape, for instance, raising my financial support. I didn't have a penny! Now negative thoughts crept in, *How can I possibly go to Guatemala for a year? I've got to raise all that support.* Summer was fast approaching and all I had so far were a few contacts. My life was already extremely busy from now till the end of the school year, studying for finals and getting ready for graduation.

I had planned on spending that summer helping my brother in revivals. He would be speaking in some camp meetings and churches where I could possibly present my support needs. Still, I was a bit discouraged. I had told all my friends and other people my plans. Many were praying for me, but none were making pledges for support. Nothing was happening.

During the last month of school I was the song leader for our Foreign Mission Society. I surely didn't feel much like leading the singing that last meeting of the school year. The president stood up to encourage us about going to the mission field. Well, I wanted to go alright, but I didn't have any money. So his message left me feeling worse, rather than encouraged.

As the service was ending, the president said, "We have a special announcement." I was sitting on the platform not paying much attention. "One of our members is going to Guatemala." Up came my head and I was listening! "Yes, one of our members here, Brother Don, our song leader and preacher, is going to Guatemala for a year. So the Foreign Missions Society board has authorized me to give a donation of $600 dollars for his support." Oh my friends, could you believe it, in one moment I had $600 dollars for my support! In those days that was a *lot* of money. I was overjoyed! I felt so ashamed for doubting God's providence, but God now confirmed that it was going to be alright. I was going to get the necessary support.

That was just the beginning. Providence planned more. As I left Lon Morris, all I had was an old 1954 Ford with an oil leak and lots of miles to cover that summer. That old Ford and I made it to a little town in Michigan to a church my brother had arranged for me. They decided they would support me. I was thrilled. As I traveled that whole summer, at every church my support began to come in. And that little old Ford, with its oil leak, kept on running. I attended two camp meetings where Bud was the evangelist and raised more, so that by the end of summer I had most of my support. That was a great burden that the Lord lifted. He also arranged for Global Harvesters Foundation Inc. to take care of my book-keeping. Global Harvesters had no overhead expenses, so every penny that was designated for me went to my work in Guatemala.

Next I was invited to participate in a mission conference in Shreveport, LA, at the church that Bud's wife had attended. It was one of those big independent charismatic churches. I pulled that old Ford up in front of the church to get ready for the evening services. A man came running up to me. *Uh, oh, he's going to ask me to move my old junk-heap.* Instead he said, "Brother Don, I understand you're going to Guatemala." He looked at my beat-up Ford and said, "You are not going to drive *that* down there are you?" Hah, I didn't even know you *could* drive down to Guatemala.

Honestly, I hadn't even *thought* about how I was getting to Guatemala. Then he said, "What you need is a nice vehicle, if you are going to drive down." Suddenly, it seemed set in cement that I *was* driving to Guatemala. I was in a dilemma. What should I say? Should I admit I hadn't considered such a basic matter as transportation? Maybe he'd think such a dolt wasn't competent enough to be a foreign missionary.

But he startled me again, "Don't worry about a thing, we'll take care of it right now. Come on, I'll take you down to my friend who has a used car lot two blocks from the church." We jumped in my car and drove to the used car lot. He hailed his friend, "Hey, this is my friend. He's going to Guatemala as a missionary. He needs another vehicle. How much will you give him for that Ford?" I just stood there, mouth agape. I hadn't decided to sell my car! This fellow was offering my car and this other man was saying "Yeah, well, I'll give him $300 for it." "Sold!" Before I even realized what was going on, I had sold my car!

I signed my title over to that man and put the $300 in my pocket. But here I was in Louisiana without a vehicle. We walked back to the church where he had his car. It was nice of him to help, but I didn't think I was going to get very far with $300 in my pocket.
I was more bewildered when he said, "Now, come on, let's go find you a good vehicle." Oh sure. With $300. Anyway, I had no idea what type of car I would need to drive to Guatemala—to a place where I hadn't even known I *could* drive till an hour ago?

Well, I guess this brother was being led by the Spirit, because he drove right to a Volkswagen dealer. "Where is a salesman? I want to know if you have any of those little buses, those Volkswagen Kombis?" "Right now, we don't have one." "Well how long would it take you to get one?" The salesman looked at his book and exclaimed "Say! The boat from Germany is docking today in New Orleans and two on that boat belong to us here." My friend asked, "Could you have one up here by tomorrow afternoon?" "I sure can!" the salesman exclaimed. "How much?" The total price would be $3,600.00. They made the deal. In a daze, I handed over my $300.00 for a down payment.

He then said, "Now, come on, let's go see the pastor." I wondered if he was hoping for a miracle-on-demand. He told me that Jack Moore was the co-pastor of this church. He was also a contractor, with his own company building houses, one of these men who liked to work, get his hands dirty. We found him in a house that he was building over in another part of town.

Dressed in his overalls, Pastor Jack was sawing some boards. He stopped, greeted us. My friend said, "Bro Jack, you know this is Bro Don. He is going to Guatemala as a missionary." Bro. Jack said, "Yes, yes we're praying for him, for the Lord to bless him." "Well, Bro Jack, he needs an automobile! We found just the right vehicle, a Volkswagen Kombi. What we need is $3,300 to buy it."

Bro Jack put down his saw, brushed his hands off on his overalls, reached into that big front pocket, took out his checkbook, got his pen out and wrote a check to me for $3,300! He handed it to me, saying, "Son, go and get yourself an automobile. You pay me back whenever you can." And that was it. Now I had $3,600 toward an automobile that I hadn't even known I wanted to buy.

The next day the dealer had a brand-new, shiny Kombi, right off the boat from Germany. We gave the man the check. He gave me the keys. My friend said, "Well, praise the Lord, you got you a good vehicle. Have a good trip to Guatemala!" Off he drove. Friends, I was left standing there with my head swirling. I wasn't quite sure what had transpired, it had all happened so fast.

So I took off in my new Kombi for the rest of my summer, up north for meetings, then back to Kentucky before heading to Guatemala.

I had told Virgil Zapata that I would arrive in Guatemala about the first of September to help with the school closing. Their school year ended in October and started again in January.

CRAMPED KOMBI

After the summer meetings, I was thankful for a bit of time before heading to Guatemala. I opened another letter from Virgil. Virgil wrote an urgent request: "We have some supplies that need to be brought down. They are in Atlanta, Georgia. Do you think you might be able to swing by there and pick those things up and bring them with you to Guatemala?" Uh oh, there goes my *breathing space*. Well, at least I now owned a bus with plenty of room.

I drove to the mission in Atlanta and met the president of the mission, Bro Glen Dicks. My, I couldn't believe that I was meeting such a fine missionary. I stayed for a couple of days with Bro Glen, already beginning to feel a bit like a missionary.

Then Glen showed me the supplies for the school in Guatemala--a washing machine, 15 cases full of books and papers, paraphernalia for the mimeograph machine, bottled ink, cleansers, Bibles. You name it, it was there. Was my Kombi big enough for all of it?

I got right to work and packed that Volkswagen bus until I didn't think I could put another inch of stuff in. Whew, got it all in. Oops. I discovered I had to take *ten* sheets of Formica, four by eight, to put on the tables at the dormitory dinning hall of the school. I managed to slide those in on top without ripping the bus headliner. Now I was ready to leave for Guatemala.

Then it hit me that I was *really* going to drive all the way to Guatemala! I began to think it would be awfully nice to have some help driving. I had never even driven in Mexico! Again, God's provision had gone ahead of me. A few months earlier I had stopped in Robinson, IL, to preach and present the Guatemala ministry. I had stayed with a good friend of mine, Aubrey Long. He was a truck driver. Wouldn't a professional driver be a terrific companion? So I called him. "Do you think you could take a week off and drive with me down to Guatemala?" He quickly replied, "I sure will."

Now I had professional support, but Aubrey admitted that he had never been anywhere outside of the U.S. in his life. O.K. We were even, both clueless as to what we were headed for. We met in Dallas, TX, where my folks were pastoring. From there we took off in our Cramped Kombi, heading for Guatemala. And the unknown.

ON THE ROAD

What a beginning we had to our great adventure! We arrived at the border station in Brownsville. The Mexican officials took one look at my Volkswagen full of all that stuff, immediately informing me, "You will have to declare what you have there, pay a bond, which will be returned to you when you cross our southern border." I couldn't speak Spanish, so wasn't sure what they were telling me, except that they weren't letting me into Mexico.

They understood some English and finally got it through to me that I must make a list of *everything* in the Kombi! Oh no, unpack all that stuff I'd just crammed in? We had no choice. They examined it all, made sure it was all on that list. Then I had to pay a bond and re-stuff it all back into the Kombi.

Finally, we were driving through Mexico. That was in 1959 and the roads in Mexico were not at all like they are today. Enough said. Next stop was in Tuxtla Gutiérrez to pick up Bill Cook, another missionary headed for the school in Guatemala. I pulled into the hotel at Tuxtla Gutiérrez at 10 o'clock at night, found his room, knocked on the door. He was on the phone talking to Stu Bundy in Guatemala. Connections were obviously not very good, so he was hollering at the top of his voice. What language was he speaking? I didn't understand a word of what was being said. Turned out it was Spanish, but his native Argentinean variety of

Spanish. What sort of conversations could we patch together during our our long trip together?

Regardless, the next day the three of us journeyed on through Mexico, headed toward the border of Guatemala. It seemed forever till we finally arrived at the southern Mexico border control station. More endless paperwork and negotiations. They did refund my bond money, but it was around midnight when we finally cleared Mexico.

It began to rain just as we were heading into a stretch of one of the most treacherous roads in Guatemala. We were navigating a dirt road under construction, but not finished. It had just opened to vehicles that very month. There were very few bridges. In places where the water was running across the road, we stopped so one of us could get out, wade into the water and find the shallowest part to cross. Alas, it didn't get better--the roads were muddy all the way to about twenty miles from Guatemala City.

We drove into Guatemala City around five p.m., just in time to witness a major street demonstration, with tear gas filling the air. It was apparently something against the government. Police on horseback were trying to break it up. That was my first experience of Guatemala City, a riot in the streets with tear gas burning my eyes. And me wondering *What in the world am I getting into? Welcome to the mission field, Don.*

It turned out to be a good year. I learned Spanish, assisted the school and interacted with lots of Guatemalan kids. The Kombi helped transport the school's singing quartet all the way to San Jose, Costa Rica. At the end of my year in Guatemala I sold the Kombi to some missionaries for $3,300.00. Upon my return to the USA I went back to that church in Shreveport, found Bro Jack, thanked him, and gave him a check for $3,300.00. He gave me a big hug, put the check in his pocket and simply said, "Blessings on you, Bro Don. Thank you." He didn't linger to be praised. He had been God's humble provision for my transportation to learn Spanish in Guatemala.

CHARMING SENORITA

During that year in Guatemala, God added other goals to my plans. First, He let me know He wanted me long-term in Guatemala. That was fine. I liked that beautiful country. But the truly astounding part of God's plan was when He revealed to me the great need for an aviation ministry there! Had I *really* thought I had completely given up my love of flying when I answered His call to missions?

But for this year, my assignment was to spend my time learning Spanish. I was boarding with two young men from The Evangelical Schools of Latin America ministry. Through them and the surrounding evangelical community, I met many great Christians, including the Perez family. The family was highly respected in the community, including their son and three extremely lovely daughters. The oldest girl was two years younger than I, the next five years younger, then came the brother, seven years younger. The youngest girl was just a kid, eight years younger than myself.

But would you believe, they also boarded five other young ladies who were administrators and teachers with the mission! Wow! Things were certainly looking up for me to find a good Christian wife! Imagine being surrounded by eight young ladies! Since our weekly mission meetings were held at the Perez home, I got to see them all frequently–in a wonderful atmosphere--with good food, too.

I learned that the two older Perez girls were planning to go to the U.S. to attend Bob Jones University. I didn't know the son or youngest daughter's future plans. They were teenagers and probably didn't know, either. I caught glimpses of this daughter but had no opportunity to talk to her, since she was too young to take part in our meetings. Even those glimpses made me sit up and notice that she had sparkling brown eyes and long black hair. I thought to myself W*hen that girl grows up, she is going to be a beautiful woman.*

My two roommates invited me to an evangelical church for a major Hispanic cultural event, a fiesta de quince años, a girl's 15th birthday celebration. Since I was so desirous of learning the culture of Latin America, I happily accepted this event. Even better, it was in honor of the youngest Perez daughter. The event turned out to be a regular service with a nice message.

She and her parents sat in the front of the church. She was dressed up with gloves, hat and high heels.

Afterwards, we were all invited to the Perez house for a time of celebration with some of her classmates. Even with a language barrier, surrounded by so many young ladies, how could I not have a good time? The honoree greeted me with formal politeness. Even though that seemed rather icy, amid that swarm of femininity, I was smitten by this one young lady! I had a strong sense that I was going to marry her someday. But how could that *possibly* be, with that eight year difference in our ages?

For now I was headed back to Kentucky for my first year of seminary.

BARNSTORMING BLUNDER

With conviction that God would provide, I made my first major purchase, a Cessna 180 plane that I would need for ministry in Latin America. However, with no checks from Bro Jack this time, I would be making payments for quite some time.

During the first summer's break from seminary I was scheduled for a full slate of revivals in southern Indiana, Illinois, and Kentucky. Though I was eager to begin flying my new plane for ministry, none of my scheduled locations had nearby landing fields. So I drove to a rural church in Indiana to start a two week evangelistic crusade.

A very nice family had invited me to stay with them on their farm. As I drove in I noticed, right next to the house, a long hay field with a fence at one end and a row of small trees at the other end. It had a gradual slope from the fence down to the row of trees. Looked good. On Monday, I asked the farmer if I could fetch my airplane and land there. He thought that would be just fine, so I drove back to Kentucky for the plane. I flew in and landed, no problem.

As an enticement to attract youth to that revival, I invited them to 'come on out' for an 'Old Fashioned Plane Washing.' On Saturday afternoon we served hotdogs, hamburgers and drinks. After that, we all washed and waxed the plane. The unique event brought a good turnout. The crusade ended well with many touched by the Gospel message.

As I was preparing my takeoff, I discovered I had made a terrible mistake. I didn't have enough room to clear those small trees! Takeoff in the other direction needed only to clear a small fence, but that was uphill-- out of the question—my plane couldn't take off uphill. I was stuck! My host said, "Don't worry, I'll get my chainsaw and we'll cut down enough trees for your wings to fit through!" I shed my shirt and got right to work to clear an opening in the trees for takeoff.

This brought to mind the early days of aviation when pilots flew out to rural areas to display their newfangled machines. Full of bravado, many pilots were eager to show off their skills and daring. Barnstorming became a crowd-gasping favorite, flying in one large door of a barn and (hopefully) out the other.

Sadly, I was born too late to be part of those exciting times. However, I felt as if I was just about to find myself doing something similar, try to fly through that 'door' we had cut in the trees. Whew! We had removed enough trees! I flew through with no problem.

Enter another problem. Unbeknown to me, that fence row where we had cut down the trees was full of poison ivy! The next day I flew to Illinois to start a two week revival. It was hot and humid in church that night. Though it was summer, in those more formal days I wore a long sleeve white shirt and tie. Oh, I began to ITCH!

In my room that night I found I was covered with great red welts all over my torso. The next day I could hardly preach! I was trying valiently to keep from scratching in public. With the added heat of day, I began perspiring profusely, causing the welts to burn. Somehow I did manage to preach and I did survive the experience. So it was onward to Kentucky for a ten day revival.

Wherever I preached I was on the lookout for landing sites. When I found one near a church where I was to preach, I secured advance permission to land. My strategy was to have the church announce a 'Mission Airplane Rally' for the Sunday afternoon I would arrive. Then when I flew in there I'd land in the field, conduct a service, pray for the plane and my future flying plans in Latin America. An actual plane in a farmer's field created a good visual aid for donations to help me pay for the airplane.

To raise more for the airplane fund, I utilized another skill God had been developing. I had sharpened my singing talents over the years as the song evangelist in my brother's revivals. So I recorded a vinyl LP album of hymns. The album was entitled "Hymns North and South of the Border." On one side I recorded six hymns in Spanish, six hymns on the other side in English. With a donation of any amount for the airplane fund, an album was yours.

When preaching in Kentucky, a dear lady came up to me and said, "Brother Don, that record I got is bad. I can not understand a word you're singing!" Chuckling to myself, I kindly told her, "Sister, you have to turn it over to hear the songs in English." As I went to other revival locations, I thought of the reverse side of the album and hoped that Spanish-speakers could understand songs sung in my early-days Spanish 101.

CHIQUI, A LOVE STORY

This love story might have begun years earlier, with a different name in that title. After all, I had been enrolled in Asbury College, a Christian college known humorously as "a shoe factory"—uniting a guy and a gal, then sending them out in "pairs." It was an ideal place for a young preacher boy to find his mate, since there were many young ladies looking for young preacher boys. But I was headed for the mission field.

50

Alas, not many of the females on campus wanted a life quite that adventurous. So when I graduated still single, it seemed to me that my chances of finding a suitable wife were greatly diminished.

When my year in Guatemala came to an end, I had learned Spanish but, even surrounded by those eight senoritas, I returned as a bachelor to Kentucky to continue my education at seminary. Once again, my life was busy, involved in school and evangelism with my older brother.

Then came Asbury Seminary's winter quarter, not a good time for local evangelical meetings. So I decided to take those three months to return to Guatemala. Since I had made many contacts while there, I would have sufficient opportunities to preach. This plan proved effective and continued during several seminary winter quarters

One winter quarter I inquired as to how the Pérez family was doing. As you might suspect, my interest was mainly in the youngest daughter. I hadn't seen her for a few years. I learned she was studying to be a nutritionist and had gone to Ohio to study at a Bible college. I wasn't pleased to think of her surrounded by young men at that Bible school. Hmm. Obviously my interest in her wasn't exactly casual.

When I had some preaching assignments in churches in southern Ohio, I called her to check on how she was doing. I told her I was in the area and thought it would be nice if I could come by and visit with her. She informed me that it would be impossible due to the strict regulations of that Bible college. Only family members were allowed to visit the students. What a disappointment, as well as a danger—me shut out and her 'shut in' with all those Bible college young men.

Back in Guatemala a year later, I heard that she was home. By now, it had been about six years since I had seen her. She would be a lovely, grown-up young lady. Miraculously none of those eligible Bible college men had 'caught' her. Then it hit me that I now had considerable *Guatemalan* competition! The Perez girls were not only beautiful, but considered to be top-notch in evangelical circles. Inquiring discretely, I discovered I would be in the back of a discouragingly long line. Quite a few impressive young men had the same intentions as I had. They included a young Guatemalan evangelist, a pastor's son, an architect, a doctor and the brother-in-law of her older sister who lived next door to her. Chances were looking mighty dark for me.

Well, I had waited all these years. I was *not* going to give up now. She *was* to be mine. Over the years I had been invited to speak at her church. Now I gladly accepted an invitation to speak there, knowing that the Perez family would certainly attend. As I sat up on the platform during the singing, I scanned the congregation to see if I could spot her. Ah, there was her mother and, sitting next to her, an incredibly beautiful twenty-two year old. Believe me, it was hard to preach! I could not keep my eyes off of her.

After the service, as is my custom, I stood at the door to greet all the people (including one young lady).

First came her father, Don Jose Luis, very cordial, then her mother, Doña Esther. Ah yes, her mother suspected my intentions, but she greeted me kindly. Then at last my Heart's Desire stood beside me! I took her hand in mine--for the first time!

This was the moment 1 had been waiting and dreaming of. Here she was and I was speaking to her. I knew that this was D-Day (do or die), so I said to her, "Could I come by the house to see you?" I was stunned to hear her answer "No." I could not believe it! Not only had I *never* been turned down before, but this "no" shattered my dreams. I felt desperate, so I said, "Can I call you on the phone?" The same answer, a polite "No." I pulled myself together for my last-ditch effort. "Well, Can I write to you?" With a shoulder shrug, she answered, "If you wish." It appeared that I was being shown the exit door.

Still, I couldn't give up. I prayed for another opportunity. Oddly, it came indirectly through the Presbyterian Church and missionary friends I had stayed with when in Guatemala before. They had established the first Christian camp for youth in Central America. It was located about five miles south of the city on a beautiful lake. The camp had a peaceful landscape, cabins for the campers and a swimming pool, a real rarity in those days. Currently I was staying in the beautiful main house overlooking the lake with John Shakleford and and his wife. As a guest, I could use the pool, since there were no camp sessions at that time of year.

Suddenly a brilliant thought popped into my mind. The brother of my Heart's Desire was an Eagle Scout, a great outdoors and sports enthusiast. Aha! I called Luis and asked him if he would like to come out to the camp and go swimming. Of course he jumped at the invitation! I told him he could come that following Friday *on one condition*--he was to bring his little sister with him. I don't know what transpired at the Perez house that day, but he informed me later that he would be there on Friday--with his sister!

Luis certainly did a lot of swimming that day. He had the pool to himself. I spent all the time sitting on a bench overlooking the lake and the pool, talking to Chiqui. Yes, her name is Chiqui! Her real name is Lilia Esther. In Guatemala it is the custom to give the name nickname Chiqui (small, little one) to the youngest of the family, whether a boy or girl. Sometimes they carry these names into adulthood, as had this Chiqui. Her friends knew her by that name.

Next I was able to receive permission to visit her in her home. I began to do that as often as possible. You must understand that Chiqui was raised by her wonderful Christian parents in the old-school way of doing things known as 'guardada'. We could visit in the living room of her house, but she was not to be alone with me.

I had to learn many cultural boundaries, then abide by them! It wasn't all bad--saved money, actually. For instance, I couldn't take her out for a cup of coffee (or anywhere) unless we had a chaperone. So we did most of our courting in her living room. We would listen to some music, talking a lot, just getting to know each other. Every so often her mother would come in and ask if we wanted a drink, a cookie or something. Believe me, Mama kept a close eye on the entire situation. But it was a great way to get to know each other. I would heartily recommend it as a 'healthy recipe' for couples in the early stages of courtship.

I was gradually learning other cultural differences. For instance, being raised in a conservative Christian home, her two choices of music were Christian or classical—that was about it. Christians simply did not listen to 'worldly' music, especially the mariachi music so popular in all of Latin America. One day in a bookstore I found an album of music entitled, "Enamorado de ti." (I am in love with you). Recorded by a very popular Mexican singer, it was not exactly appropriate, but the title so well stated how I felt. Chiqui's parents allowed me to present it to her, assuming that I still didn't quite understand the cultural differences. I happily let it go at that. It was a way for me attempt to express my deep feelings for her.

More cultural procedures came into play during early courting days. My next step needed to be a declaration that I wanted to be her *novio*, something akin to going steady but more formal. I had go to her parents for permission to be her novio, assuring them that my attentions were for her only and that I was willing to abstain from any other relationship. I was very thankful when that permission was granted as a beginning step for us.

The next few years were very difficult, as I was in the USA and only going to Guatemala for a couple of months each year. Courting was mostly by letters. Phone calls were entirely too expensive, so totally out of the question. That was long before Internet, cellphones, laptops and other devices to maintain communication. She gave me a picture that I have even to this day on my desk. If it were possible to wear out a picture by looking at it, hers would be in shreds.

After subsequent visits to Guatemala, we were able to more firmly establish our relationship. This meant another visit to her parents to declare that my intentions were to become engaged to be married. They gave their approval, even though it was hard for Mama Esther. She just knew that I was going to take her little girl far away. She was right--that's exactly what I did.

Next, I was back to tell her parents that we were ready to set a wedding date. Once again they gave their approval. On this occasion, Don Jose Luis did want to know exactly how I was going to take care of his daughter. Financially, they knew I was supported by ministry funds. However, they had other questions, such as where we were going to live. At this particular time I was living in an Airstream Trailer. Uh, oh. In their culture the only people who lived in travel trailers were Gypsies or circus people. So I replied honestly, "Yes, I have a place for us to live, however it does have wheels." Fortunately, Papa Luis didn't put the brakes on the wedding plans. We would spend our first four years of married life living in that trailer.

Since I had firm commitments to speak at evangelistic services for the next three years, we had to scour our calendars for a date when we could get married. I discovered two weeks free during the month of February, so the decision was made--February 27th.

WEDDING DAZE

When I arrived at the airport in Guatemala for the wedding, my heart skipped a beat (lots of beats!) when I saw her coming out the door and running to meet me. It finally dawned on me, "I AM GETTING MARRIED!" After nine long years of waiting and dreaming, I knew for sure that she was mine!

Those next two weeks were extremely hectic. As is the custom, two weeks before the wedding I had to put an announcement in the official newspaper of the government. In my case, I had to state that I was a foreigner contemplating matrimony with a Guatemalan lady. This statement attested that there were no other women nor did I have children by other women. I also had to inform the U.S. Embassy of our marriage.

Next we set a date for the civil matrimony, which the law requires. On Monday we went to the municipal building for a lawyer to draw up the civil wedding arrangements, along with receiving a bit of advice about the sacredness of marriage. Then it was off to her home for a formal meal to celebrate that civil wedding. This included Chiqui's family, a few invited guests, my father and my older brother who had just arrived. After dinner, I retired back to the campgrounds where I was staying. I chuckled at the irony of bunking for two nights with my father and brother, even though I was technically a married man!

Thursday was our church wedding. For Chiqui, that was the only wedding that counted, taking our vows before God, not some government official. However, everything felt seriously rushed. We were scheduled to start a week's revival at a church in Oklahoma City on Sunday morning. Only three days after our wedding we had to be in the USA!

We were married in Guatemala City's Union Church, the largest church available at that time. The Perez' church was too small for the many invited guests. These guests even included some of my former *rivals* that Chiqui had kindly invited to usher!

Then, oh no, another cultural faux pas. I arrived for the ceremony wearing my best pair of boots. When Chiqui saw them she said, "You can't get married in boots, that's just not done here!" So I asked missionary friends if anyone had a pair of black shoes I could borrow. Fortunately, one had a pair that fit. But then came another *oops*. I didn't realize that one shoe had a hole in the sole, visible to all when we knelt at the altar to take communion with our backs to the congregation. I've often wondered how many people were thinking *Poor girl, she's marrying that penniless missionary.*

My father conducted the marriage ceremony, another preacher gave a message, followed by choir and solo music. After the celebration, we left for our first married night at the lovely Camino Real Hotel. I can still take you to the very room we had. That was it--our one-night honeymoon. I definitely do not recommend this way to begin married life! Even just another day or two of honeymoon would have been exceedingly better, but this had to suffice.

The very next day we grabbed our suitcases and caught a commercial flight to New Orleans where I had left my single engine Cessna 180. We had to jump in and fly. I don't recall if I had thought to ask Chiqui if she had ever flown in a small airplane--or even if she was nervous about it. What a gal! She just climbed right in that Cessna like she had done it before, no questions asked, as natural as you can imagine.

We were aiming for Texas, flying low over Oklahoma, what pilots called *scud running*. The cloud cover and mist had descended to very low altitudes. Even following the highway below us wasn't a safe way to fly. I did have an instrument license but it didn't help under those conditions. I called to a passing Lear Jet, trying to get a report of where we could top the clouds. His reply was, "Passing through 30,000 feet and still not on top." So we continued flying above the highway until I spotted a small airport off my starboard side. With sights of relief, we landed safely.

The airport consisted of one small building. Oddly, a group of people stood around under umbrellas.

What are all those people doing here on such a cold, cloudy day? I taxied up to the ramp. As I shut down the engine, all those people rushed over, surrounding the plane. Then the door on Chiqui's side was opened by a very elegantly dressed lady with a huge bouquet of flowers in her arms. Both of us were dumbfounded. What could all this mean? As the lady joyously thrust the flowers into Chiqui's arms, she gave us a warm welcoming speech! My new bride was now thinking *My goodness, Americans are certainly nice people to do all this to welcome us!*

At that very moment the elegant lady took a second look, pulled the flowers out of Chiqui's arms and announced in a surprised voice, "Why, you're not Miss America!" She marched the crowd back to the small building. Puzzle solution: In an incredible coincidence, the real Miss America was to fly in to visit this small Oklahoma town on that very day and hour. Chuckling, my heart told me that the *real* Miss America was sitting right next to me in the plane. In that nasty weather, I suspect that the real Miss America's plane never got there, leaving that big bouquet with 'our' welcoming committee.

After waiting for the weather to improve, we flew on to Texas. In Longview we had a quick visit with Chiqui's brother who was studying at LeTourneau College. Saturday morning we took off again for Oklahoma City. A cold front had moved in, so we were flying in snow showers and low clouds, probing our way to our destination. Chiqui never complained about flying conditions, this time, nor through all our married years. Not even the time we were snowed-in for two days in western Nebraska, fogged-in for several days in Pittsburg or dodging big tropical thunderstorms in southern Mexico with fierce turbulence.

As a matter of fact, only once has she *ever* made any comments about flying. The one time she spoke up was when we were to fly from Nebraska to Missouri, an area famously known as Tornado Alley. I had planned to leave right in the middle of a tornado watch! Hmm. She thought it *might be best* to delay our take-off, since tornado warnings had been issued all along our route!

Now just two days after our wedding, she flew with me through snow and low clouds, arriving safely in Oklahoma. The pastor, a classmate from seminary, met us and drove us to his home. The house had only two rooms and one bathroom. They had a newborn baby and a four year old girl. The little girl moved out of her room for us, but we all needed to share the one bath. The four year old, like most young children, was curious about guests in her room. She kept coming to the door to see what we were doing. Believe me, that is no way to begin married life!

Not realizing how exhausted we might be, our pastor friend informed us that he wanted to take us out that evening to a youth gathering. He thought it would be a good opportunity to meet the young people and youth director before the revival meetings began.

Off we went to church. To our astonishment, the first thing we saw was the youth director on the dance floor dancing with a young girl from the church. The event was a *sock-hop*, much like a present-day disco. Try to imagine what was going through the mind of my new bride, raised in a conservative church where *any* sort of dancing was prohibited. Now she had landed, as a new bride, in a dramatically different environment. She must have been wondering how she could get back home as soon as possible. Alas, she was too far away.

The next meetings were in a large church in Pennsylvania and the members treated us wonderfully. Blessedly, they put us up in a nice hotel near the church. We had a very enjoyable two weeks and--at last--a little privacy!

From rushed wedding days, scary flights, tightly-scheduled meetings, a four year old peeking in at our door and 'pagan' dancing, the beginning of our marriage was quite stressful, to say the least. The Lord brought us through and gave Chiqui abundant grace to put up with it all.

God has continued to bless us with so much over these wonderful fifty years! I can truthfully say Chiqui has been my true love, and my strength. I thank the Lord for giving her to me. I have often thought *She is not a woman, she is an angel in disguise.* Marrying her has been the greatest thing in my life, second only to committing my life to Jesus.

One would never have supposed that a beautiful Guatemalan señorita would top all those Christian college and seminary gals as the ideal missionary preacher's wife. She has also been a dedicated mother and grandmother, as well as a faithful servant of the Lord. I am incredibly thankful that this love story began when it did and not at Asbury's *shoe factory, paired off* with another student.

A HARD SELL

I'd come to Guatemala with great expectations of immediately flying around the country serving rural missionaries. With few roads in rural, mountainous Guatemala, travel was very difficult and time-consuming. Obviously I and my plane would be welcomed as providing a most valuable service.

With great enthusiasm, I began contacting missionaries to inform them that efficient airplane services were available. I was stunned to discover that, since they'd never had plane service before, they had no clue of the advantages of flying. It seemed I was going to have to sell them on the idea.

I never dreamed it would be so difficult. I ran into many road blocks. Time after time I'd hear, "Nobody has ever done it before." As if that were proof it shouldn't be done. Others replied that they weren't sure it wasn't God's will. Some apparently thought using planes might put their manhood in question: "I don't need an airplane. I've handled this myself for many years." Sometimes I got the response "I'm not interested but Joe Blow might be." He wasn't.

Finally, the president of Central American Mission gave me some excellent advice. "You won't get very far by just being a lone operator. I suggest that you get yourself organized, form a board, get a name and become a registered entity with the Guatemalan government."

So I decided that's what I would do. I found a Christian lawyer. We went over the details. It would be very straightforward, so I thought. It was easy to select a board: my three brothers-in-law, my father-in-law, along with others from our church. Wise and spiritual men, every one. Then as a board we began to tackle all the necessary legal requirements, such as by-laws and an official name. My lawyer said our name must contain the word 'association' because that best described our category type. Of course, it would be appropriate to have 'Guatemala', identifying us as a Guatemalan entity.

Now we had two words, 'association' and 'Guatemala'. A – G. I began to look for an acronym, since I love acronyms. I thought, "Well A, G, and of course, another A for aviation." Ah, it was beginning to resemble the Greek word AGAPE, love. Now I just needed words for the P and the E. I began to think about P words. Well, 'for' in Spanish is 'para'. Now I only lacked the letter E. Yes, the most natural word a missionary would think of—Evangelization! It was ideal. The Association Guatemalteca in Aviation Para Evangelization would describe my purposes for the organization.

There was one little catch, my lawyer told me. The Guatemalan government of those years did not look favorably on evangelical organizations. We were a very small minority in a Catholic country still steeped in prejudices against evangelicals. So he predicted, "If you put that word in there, they'll surely reject it." They did.

So I had to find another E word. In my Spanish dictionary one definition of the word ´edify´ is 'to give a good example'. That was it! That's what we wanted to do, to give a good example by helping our neighbors, reaching out to those in need. So the word edification, gave me the E, which spelled A-G-A-P-E. Who could reject love?

To my chagrin, I was informed that it was rejected again. I was puzzled about that one. So I hustled off to the National Palace to ask the man in charge of that department what was the problem. As I sat at the desk of this very important government official, he explained the reason it was rejected was "Because the name did not match what your organization proposes to do." Beg your pardon? He told me, "The definition of edification is to build something, but your by-laws do not mention anything about construction projects."

I sent up a quick prayer and waded in to tell this important Guatemala lawyer the second definition of edificación is 'to give a good example'. Amazingly, he accepted that, even from an evangelical gringo. Now I had an organization, a board, a plane, a name. We were all set to go.

But I still couldn't get missionaries interested in flying. Somehow I'd have to show them the advantages. Sell my services. I kept thinking, *I brought this plane down because I saw a real need. How is it that nobody can comprehend how much more they can accomplish if they don't have to drive long hours on rutted dirt and mud roads, slipping and sliding over steep mountain grades?*

Then one day the phone rang. It was Dick Landis, a Mennonite missionary. His ministry was located in a town called Coban. He said, "Hey Don, I hear you have an airplane. I need to get to Coban urgently. Can you take me to Coban?" My first customer! I was thrilled that, at last, I could demonstrate this valuable service! "Sure Dick, I can take you to Coban!"

There was only one problem, I didn't know where Coban was located. So I told him to meet me at 8:30am at the Aeroclub, the operations center for all private aircrafts in Guatemala. I went well ahead of time and found a couple of Guatemalan pilots. "Hey, where's Coban?" "Ah, easy," they said, "No problema, 23 minutes, 360 degrees north." In those days we didn't have a GPS, no fancy navigational radios. It was very primitive, with only compass and watch. We flew for years in the bush using our watches, following a compass. That's all we had.

So I repeated, "Just straight north, twenty-three minutes?" They said, "That's right, the airstrip is on the west side of town." I assumed there was nothing more needed, since they gave no information about the terrain, what it looked like, or what the weather was like. I had never flown in that area. I'd flown to the south, to the east, but never north. Back then I didn't know that it was famous for bad weather: "In Coban it rains thirteen months a year!" They even had a nickname for its famous drizzle—'chippi-chippi'.

Well, I had promised and the pilots had said it was easy. Dick arrived promptly. As we boarded the plane Dick asked, "Hey, how long is this going to take?" I confidently replied, "23 minutes." He was absolutely thrilled. "Wow! That's great, 'cause it takes me eight hours by car." And I thought, "Oh boy, here's my chance to really sell air service as a great tool for evangelism!"

So we took off. Beautiful, clear blue sky with a few white fluffy clouds floating around. I looked at my watch, put my compass on 360 degrees. This was going to be a piece of cake. I crossed the first ridge north of Guatemala City at about 25 miles at 8,500 – 9,000 feet, with good visibility. Ahead I saw another beautiful, but higher, mountain range. I didn't worry about what was up there, over there, nor what Coban looked like. I was concentrating on the time and compass heading. I did notice that the ridge was covered with clouds. I thought, "Well, hopefully, on the other side things will look better."

As I crossed that second ridge my heart sank. Out in front, as far as the eye could see in any direction, was a solid overcast of clouds, only a mountain peak peeping through to my right and another over to my left. *Oh no, how am I going to spot Coban through this thick cloud cover?*

I knew if I didn't make it and had to turn around, Dick would tell everybody, "Missionaries can't fly here in Guatemala. Flying is for the birds!" (Pun intended.) My career as a missionary bush pilot might be over before it began.

"Lord, help me!" I prayed fervently and started my descent at 360 degrees. My watch marked 23 minutes. We should be there. I looked down but all I could see were clouds in every direction. I leaned across to look out Dick's window and, lo and behold, there was a little hole in the clouds. Looking down that hole I saw several streets and houses, a Central Park. Of course, it could be *any* town. I wouldn't know Coban even if I landed smack dab in the middle of it! Nonetheless, there was *some* town there. I banked the plane to that side so that Dick could look down into that hole.

But how could I *possibly* ask Dick if that was Coban without revealing that I was lost? Just then Dick looked out the window, through that hole in the clouds, and shouted, "Hey, that's Coban!" "Oh, thank you Lord!" I shut the engine down, pulled her back and started spiraling down through that hole. I just wanted to land in Coban as soon as possible.

But you should never go spiraling through a cloud hole without knowing what's down there. I soon discovered what was down there. Coban sits in a valley, a 'bowl' surrounded by mountains in every direction. I was now trapped, flying around inside that bowl, covered by those clouds. How could I locate where to set the plane down safely?

At least it *was* Coban. Scanning frantically, to the west I spotted what looked like a flat area—could it be the landing strip? Well, if I was supposed to show Dick how great missionary flying is, now was the time. So I nervously headed for that flat spot. It was just grass, but it was worn off so you could see the white clay soil of a rural landing strip. I circled it once, saw no big potholes and landed. Whew, I could breathe again. *Thank you, once again, Lord!*

Dick was thrilled, "I can't believe it, we got here in 23 minutes and I would have been driving for eight hours, all day long, just to get here!" He thanked me profusely and walked off to his mission office.

As I watched him go, I thought, *Well, I've made my first flight as a missionary pilot with my first passenger. I won't have to sell my services. Dick will do it for me!*

WORDLESS MESSAGES

During an earlier trip to Guatemala I had learned that a missionary used his plane primarily to distribute tracts from the air in rural areas of Guatemala. We became acquainted and I made several flights with him, observing his ministry firsthand. Through him I gained information concerning aviation in Guatemala that would prove valuable when I came back with my own plane.

Tragically, on my next trip I discovered that he had been killed in an accident. Flying over a village, his plane hit the corner of a house and crashed. His wife and daughter had returned to the United States.

When I eventually arrived in Guatemala with my airplane, I decided that I would include tract distribution as a part of my ministry. In plastic envelopes I put a coupon for a Bible correspondence course and a booklet of the Gospel of John. My aim was to spread these over rural areas of Guatemala as I flew on other missions.

On a trip to the States I realized I was near the offices of World Missionary Press in Indiana. This ministry produced thousands of tracts in many different languages. I stopped by one day to see if they might have something that I could use. I did find a tract with the title Socorro de lo Alto (Help from Above). A perfect word-connection to distribution from an airplane above! I ordered many of the booklets in

Spanish, taking them back to Guatemala and tossing them into villages from my plane.

Some time later I met a missionary with Wycliffe Bible Translators. He asked me if I was the one who was distributing tracts from the air in the rural areas of Guatemala. Yes, I was the one. He replied that in the particular area where I was dropping those tracts, over 60% of the people did not know how to read or write! What a shock. I had been wasting all that time, money, gas and energy distributing material that almost no one could read.

Well, something must be done! Those people needed to know the Gospel. So I went home and began to sketch out a tract with pictures that would show a person how to find Jesus--without words. I didn't find it easy. But I kept sketching and finally managed to come up with something that I felt would work. Now as I flew and dropped these new tracts, I prayed the message would be understood through the pictures. (See a copy of this tract in photo section)

After distributing many of the wordless tracts, I discovered that these had become effective in a way I had never imagined. They were being used as visual aids by the native Indian evangelists who traveled between remote villages. These unsung heroes weren't even recognized by society. They lived out in the mountains, walking tirelessly over the hills, evangelizing in the dialect of their own people. They would arrive in a village, gather men, women and children around to 'show and tell' the gospel story using my tract as a visual aid. Those roving disciples are wonderful servants of God.

Later when teaching at our Bible school, I told the students about those heroic Indian evangelists. I used them as examples of how many different methods can effectively be used in evangelism. A lady who had taken my evangelism course rushed up to me at church one Sunday morning. She was really excited to tell me a story she had heard while listening to the Christian radio station. On the program pastors were invited to give their testimonies of how they had come to know the Lord and entered into the ministry.

That day a pastor began his radio testimony saying that, as a young boy, he lived in a village far up into the mountains. There was no church in his village so he had no knowledge of the gospel. One day an airplane flew over his village dropping out little leaflets. He ran and picked up one, looked at the pictures and struggled to understand what it was about. He couldn't figure it out but kept the leaflet.

After he finished primary school, since there was no high school in his village, he went to another village to continue his studies. It was there that a fellow student explained to him what those pictures meant. So when he was about 14 years old this young man gave his heart to the Lord through that little tract. After high school he went to the city and studied theology at the Bible Institute of the Central American Mission, becoming a pastor.

He added to his story, "I don't know who that man was that flew over my village that day dropping those tracts. I would love to be able to thank him. I don't know whether he is still alive or not but someday I will see him in Heaven, and I will thank him there." Oh praise the Lord forever!

TUNED-IN TO TELEVISION

In God's perfect timing, I had taken up residence in Guatemala in 1959, the same year the first television programs were broadcast. TV sets were flying off the shelves. Guatemalan TV was just in its beginning stages, on the air only a few hours each day-- in black and white, of course. All programming was managed by the government.

A young entrepreneur became interested in this new medium. As an evangelical believer, he wanted to put together a program to present the gospel on live TV. It should be inspirational with an emphasis on the importance of ethics in society. His planned format was for a learned Christian professor from one of the universities to sit at a desk giving his discourses. But he began to wonder if that would capture enough viewer interest.

This is where I tune-in. I was just a young gringo still trying to settle in, struggling with learning Spanish. But I had so far communicated well enough in church services with my chalk art. The entrepreneur had seen me draw and realized this might be a good adjunct to his program. He asked if I would do chalk drawings on his new program. I wouldn't have to a say a word, just draw--in black and white, of course.

I'd have to perform live, with no pre-taping in those days. I was thankful for the opportunity. Thus for the very first time in Guatemala an evangelical TV program went on air, regularly produced by this faithful entrepreneur.

On one occasion, the program to follow ours was to feature the mayor of Guatemala City. He would describe the advances made during his administration. While awaiting his turn on air, he stood just behind the cameras focused on me. Impressed with my drawing, he managed to get the message to me while I was drawing, "I want you to draw a picture of our new City Hall." Fortunately, I had driven by that new building every day, admiring its new style of architecture. So on camera, in front of the mayor and other ministers of the government, I drew City Hall. They were very pleased.

Skip ahead many years to the 1970's. The government of Guatemala became alarmed at the overwhelming abundance of soap operas on television. Both of the major channels aired soap operas from about six in the evening until the ten o'clock news. These programs were produced in Venezuela, Mexico and Spain, with a great amount of immoral activity portrayed openly. Those programs were watched by nearly every household in Guatemala.

The government decided that something must be done to stop this proliferation of filth corrupting the minds of Guatemala's younger generation. Thus was born Channel 5, dedicated to cultural and educational topics. The military was put in charge of the station to oversee its moral and cultural programming. Our Uncle Fernando (my wife's uncle) was appointed to head up this station. He was well-educated and one of the highest ranking officers in the entire Guatemalan military. He was a good choice because of his special interest in the arts and cultural issues.

Now some problems arose as to how to find good programming for this new endeavor. Without satellite dishes, we couldn't just link into other broadcast stations' programming. Also the government had passed a law to combat the soap operas. It stated that a certain percentage of programing must be produced locally. That left poor Uncle Fernando desperately looking for material to fill up even the few hours of those early-days broadcasting.

He called one day and asked if I would be interested in producing and presenting a program using my drawing skills. He had seen my chalk talks in church services and other events. Could I do that on television? My first response was, "Can I preach?" He replied, "Yes, you can do anything you want to do and it will not cost you a dime. The government will put it on this channel for free. Would you do a thirty minute program Monday thru Friday at 5:30 pm?"

What an opportunity to present the gospel! So I responded in the affirmative. I would target my program for children and call it "El Mundo Fascinante del Dibujo." (The Fascinating World of Art.) So we began.

By now, programs were being pre-taped. However, I hadn't taken into consideration the extensive time required to tape five programs every week. I soon realized that, with flying every day and preaching on weekends, it was just too much. I was being worn to a frazzle (a good southern expression). I inquired if I could just do a program Monday, Wednesday and Friday, instead of every day. That was agreed upon. Now every two weeks I went to the studio, located on a military base in the north part of town, to record the programs. It took hours to do the six-program recordings. I remember my drawing paper getting so hot from the production lights that it was almost impossible to touch.

The format itself was simple. With recorded music in the background, I drew and presented a message with children in mind. Occasionally I invited musicians to appear live on the show, playing or singing. Since I specialized in drawing people, I started out with illustrations from Genesis and ended up in Revelations. In the three years that I had the program I illustrated the entire Bible! Sadly, today I do not have one single tape of my productions. The station didn't have a big budget so they re-used the same tapes, recording over programs for the next set of programs.

To be true to the cultural purposes of Channel 5, once in a while I threw in teaching some aspect of art: how to draw trees, faces, hands, arms etc. On several occasions I had contests to see who could duplicate my drawing. Kids were invited to paint a picture like mine and send it to the station. I would select the best. The winners came to the studio, family in tow. They were introduced on television, received a set of paints and a nice Bible, then drew with me on the show. The response was tremendous. Kids all over Guatemala were drawing biblical stories!

The most difficult drawings of all were in a series on the twelve disciples of the Lord. The challenge was that, since we obviously do not have much information from which to depict some of the disciples, I had to use my imagination. Well, at least no one could say, "That doesn't look like him!"

To wind up that disciple series we put all twelve drawings on a special board and I gave a full message on all of the disciples. According to reports, we had many viewers that night--not just kids, but entire families were watching.

At Christmas and Easter I did special programs with my brother-in-law, a highly recognized artist in Guatemala. Since he paints scenery in oils, we combined our two mediums to present unique pictures for those special holidays. He painted a background in acrylics, which dry very fast under hot lights, then I added the figures in chalk.

By the early eighties, all those marvelous witnessing opportunities evaporated. The country's civil war was at its worst. It was decided that I should take my family out of Guatemala for a while. So, off our family sped to the jungles of Ecuador where I would fly with Mission Aviation Fellowship for one term. (The Amazing Amazon)

On our return to Guatemala six years later, we found an entirely different media. Cable television had come in like gangbusters. No one was producing local shows. After all, how could we local folk compete with the Discovery Channel, Disney, and CNN? Even Channel 5 was headed up by someone else and getting most of its programs off the dish on top of their building. Thus I was **Tuned-out of Television**.

ANGELS IN CLOUDS!

This incident happened during one of my intermittent trips to the USA from our home in Guatemala. These long treks were undertaken to preach in evangelistic campaigns, while also presenting the Guatemala mission work. This time I was thrilled that my whole family was with me, Chiqui and our two girls, four and three years old. As as this story begins we were preaching in southern Illinois, having wonderful meetings which the Lord was blessing.

Now it was time for me to fly us to Lancaster, PA, for a weekend revival. On Wednesday I checked the weather for our trip. Uh oh. It seemed the entire eastern coast was under a blanket of clouds with a stalled cold front. Every major city on the East Coast was indicating low clouds, drizzle and poor visibility. I opted to proceed with plans, hoping that, as we traveled east, the weather would clear up ahead of us, so we could arrive before Friday when the revival meetings began.

Alas, we were able to reach Pittsburgh, but no further. We trooped off to a hotel to wait for better flying weather. By Friday morning there still had not been any change in the forecast. I made the decision to carry on, filing a flight plan from Pittsburgh to Lancaster.

We took off, but I soon found myself in dense clouds with no hope of getting on top for better visibility. The mission plane I was flying under Guatemalan registry had no autopilot, so I was 'hand-flying' the entire trip in clouds. I had to monitor the gauges and keep changing the frequency on the radio. Extremely stressful multi-tasking. The weather was still not improving. At this point, I had no option except to continue on. In more ways than one, the situation was getting very dark--it would soon be night.

I was nearly out of options. Lancaster, our destination, was reporting minimum conditions for landing. 'Minimum conditions' is a critical point. Below that, you are not authorized to even *attempt* an approach. In other words, go somewhere else. But we had no other place to go. Every airport was reporting minimums--Philadelphia, Washington, Baltimore, New York--the whole East Coast was socked in.

Amid piloting tasks, something kept 'needling' my mind--the reason for my bad decision-making. I had a disease, one far too common among pilots. The disease I was suffering from is called "Get-home-itis" and has killed many, many pilots. It's a strong desire to reach a destination, *no matter what.* A very dangerous disease. Here I was, focusing on the revival meeting starting tonight at seven o'clock and feeling I *must* be there, regardless of weather.

Now the radio crackled. Whew. I didn't know words could sound so delicious. I was to report to the tower at Lancaster for landing instructions! I quickly did and they radioed the altitude for me to start the approach. What they didn't realize was that the only instrument my plane had for landing was a localizer. It would indicate if I was in line with the runway but it would not give me any altitude correction. Could I mentally gauge my altitude in this pea soup? A feeling of hopelessness began to settle over me, now combined with real panic.

Nothing to do but pray and start my descent. At that moment our four year old daughter exclaimed, "Look, Mommy, I see angels in the clouds!" *What on earth?* "Quick, Chiqui, look out and tell me if you can see anything." The very second that I heard her say, "Yes, I see something," I glanced out my window. Horror of horrors! Right ahead, only about fifteen feet below my wheels, were high-powered tension wires leading up to a large tower! Instantly I went to full climbing-power, pulled back on the wheel, almost physically straining to help the plane to climb. Just in time, I felt the plane begin to respond and pull up. Oh,

Lord, what a horrible near miss! With my entire family aboard.

Still shaking, but knowing we were safe for the moment, I called the tower and told them that I was executing a missed approach. The operator responded in a surprised voice. "What happened to you? You disappeared from our radar!" I could tell by his voice he was greatly relieved to know that we were still in the air. He gave instructions for a second approach which meant I first had to climb back into the dense gray clouds.

Before I started back, I radioed the tower operator to confess the reason for my nearly fatal mistake. I had forgotten to give him vital information regarding my plane. It did not have a 'Marker Beacon Receiver'. On approaching an airport an electronic beacon broadcasts its beam straight up in the air at about three miles from the airport. This beacon, called the 'outer marker beacon', sends a signal to the plane's Marker Beacon Receiver. That tells the plane the point where you must start to descend for landing. My plane didn't have this, since in Guatemala we don't use those beacons. Without a receiver, neither I nor my plane had known where to begin descent.

This time around, you can be sure that I asked the controller to please inform me when I crossed that beacon! On my second approach, he did. I soon saw the 'rabbit,' a series of high-powered lights that flash in sequence guiding a plane right up to the threshold of the runway. I felt the tightness straining my shoulders ease as the plane touched down!

Night, too, had touched down at the Lancaster airport. Dimly we spotted a group of folks from the church waiting for us. We grabbed our belongings, jumped in a car and took off for the church. We arrived there five minutes before church time! Chiqui took the girls to get them ready for church. I grabbed a tie and coat, my drawing equipment and headed for the platform. My legs were still shaking. Adrenaline had been flowing for hours, so I was a nervous wreck. Blessedly, the service began with singing praises to the Lord. During that time, He comforted and calmed me, so that I was able to stand at the pulpit, draw my planned chalk-talk, declaring the gospel that evening.

What lessons did the Lord re-teach me from this experience? Well, He reminded me that even 'career missionaries' can make bad decisions, just as we all are prone to do. But if we admit our failures to Him, He will forgive us, though He may allow us to suffer consequences. If we are willing, He will use the lessons we learn in our lives.

Two examples stand out in the Bible, the lives of Abram (Abraham) and King David. Abram lied, telling Pharaoh that his wife Sarai was his sister, so she was nearly taken to be one of Pharaoh's concubines. (Genesis 12:10-2)

King David made a series of really bad decisions. He stayed around home "In the Spring when kings go off to war." (II Samuel 11:1-17) Then he got a sneak-peek of Uriah's wife Bathsheba bathing and sent for her and 'laid with her'. To cover up her pregnancy, he tried to lure Uriah from the battle to have relations with his wife. That didn't work, so David sent Uriah to the front lines where he was killed.

God didn't let Abram and David's bad decisions slide by. He brought their actions to light in front of everyone. Thankfully, both confessed their sins to God, turned again to their Lord and began to live God-honoring lives.

If you are reading this story and are right now suffering under some bad decisions that you have made in life, read those biblical stories and take heart. If you turn to Him, He has promised that He will deliver you.

MINING PARADISE

My schedule was more than full. But a surprising opportunity to present the Gospel came through a large Canadian company. They had built and operated a huge nickel-mining operation next to Lake Izabal in northeastern Guatemala. With no roads to this remote area, the only way they could take out the mined product was by boat from the lake to the Caribbean Ocean.

Since this required major operations and people, they built a community for the execs and engineers. Not just temporary structures, the town had nice houses, paved streets, gardens, trees, flowers, swimming pool, restaurant and a social hall. It was a little paradise out in the rough jungle area of northeastern Guatemala.

The mining community needed a pastor. Through Union Church in Guatemala City, a request went out. Since I was a preacher and had a plane to get there, I seemed the ideal person to conduct a service every Sunday afternoon. That would work out well for me. I could be with my family on Sunday mornings, then fly up.

So the company put in a nice paved runway. Upon my arrival, they picked me up in the company car and took me to the social hall for the services. Included was always a nice meal afterwards, in air-conditioned comfort, of course. I would then fly back to the city. The company took care of all my flying expenses.

MAY DAY! MAY DAY!

After exciting adventures flying the Cessna 180 that I had brought to Guatemala in 1969, I discovered it was inadequate for many of my jobs. I decided that a Cessna 185, with more horsepower would enable me to carry bigger loads with ease. So I sold the 180 to a farmer in Belize.

I had my brother look for a good used 185 in the States. Shortly after, he located what seemed to be a nice plane with low mileage on the engine. On my next trip north, I ferried the 185 back to Guatemala. By now I had several trips across Mexico under my belt, so that long flight was becoming much easier. This trip went well with its cargo of my wife and our two little daughters. Precious cargo, indeed!

After christening my 'new' 185 with the name *La Palabra* [God's Word], I painted a Bible on the cowling. My brother-in-law, who is an artist in Guatemala, designed a stripe depicting the typical brilliant colors and weaving styles of Guatemalan Indian dress. It was quite striking and would be a testimony to all who saw it.

Cessna 185 in readiness, the mission began air service to a jungle region in the north of Guatemala that had just been opened up by the government. With many high plains Indians heading there, pastors were starting several churches. We now had the privilege of providing air transportation to those settlers and pastors.

Soon came a request to take four Norte Americanos to the city of Flores in the northern province of Peten. With the 185, that should be no problem, even though (chuckle) North Americans weigh a great deal more than Guatemalan Indians.

That day the weather in Guatemala City was beautiful with popcorn white clouds around the valley and across some of the peaks. You could see for miles. Alas, as we flew over the last ridge, the northern jungle was covered with a low layer of clouds. But at our present altitude of 8,000 feet, we were enjoying totally clear weather with a bright sun.

Now I needed to start thinking about landing at Flores. Hoping to find a hole in the clouds, I checked my watch over Coban, set my heading for 010 degrees, direct to Flores. In those days we still had no navigation aids, so reaching your destination was solely by compass and clock.

After a bit I became uneasy as I noticed that there were not any large holes below in the cloud layer. Actually, no holes of *any* size. It seemed the weather was getting thicker and not breaking up as it usually did about that time of the morning. Still, the smooth, beautiful flight was progressing and all my passengers were quite enjoying the serene cottony carpet below us.

Suddenly, with a loud BANG and tremendous vibrations, smoke filled the cabin. Then the engine lost power. Something serious had gone wrong with the engine. For a pilot the worst nightmare you can imagine is to be atop a heavy overcast with a dying engine and nothing but dense jungle below in every direction.

We had passed over the only known airfield about fifteen minutes before, too far to turn and glide back there. And Flores was still a good thirty minutes ahead. I could never glide that far. The only option was to pray and head down.

Surveying the overcast, I spied a small hole in the clouds with a river down below. But that hole was too small to get through. I couldn't head down blindly, with no idea what lay underneath. The ceiling could be anywhere from a mere 500 to 1,000 feet above the trees. Or maybe it was drizzling, with no ceiling at all!

Trying to recall a mental map of the terrain, I surmised that the river had to be the Passion River which runs north and south at this particular point. According to my watch and compass, it had to be that river. I remembered that somewhere under the overcast the Passion River makes a ninety degree turn to the left and heads for Mexico. Between that river's bend and Mexico lay an airstrip. It had to be down there, but where?

We were gliding. I had opened the windows to clear the smoke. I brought what remaining power I had back to idle, to keep the engine from vibrating off its mounts. Inside the cabin of the plane, things were really quiet. We were all praying. My prayer was simply *Lord help us get down safely, somehow.*

My stomach churned, leaving the beautiful blue sky above and entering the gray world of thick, wet clouds. Suddenly, out of nowhere, an odd thought came to me *This is just like us--the further down we let our lives sink in sin, the darker it gets.*

Don, you're the pilot! Concentrate on this crisis! What will we find when we break out of this overcast? Will we have any visibility? The plane continued sinking down and down in that dark ooze. Each tense moment only punctuated the other thought running through my mind: *Is death waiting for us down there?*

An eternity later, I finally got a glimpse of the terrain below. As I suspected, nothing but jungle, dark, foreboding, wet jungle. I cried out again to the Lord with all my heart and soul, *Lord Jesus, help us!* At least I now could see we had about a 1000-foot ceiling and it wasn't raining. I searched the terrain frantically for any sort of clearing.

Suddenly my eyes fell on a site that was almost impossible to believe! There *right in front of me* was the long grass strip of Sayaxche! All I had to do was make a slight turn on final and down we came--a nice smooth landing on the only airstrip within fifty miles! Technically, it was way too far for us to have glided from an altitude of 8,000 feet. Yet, there it was--the only airstrip, right in front of us! A miracle, yes! But now we were stuck with a disabled plane in remote Sayaxche.

When the engine had first quit, I had called "MAY DAY, MAY DAY!" (international distress signal) on the only radio frequency in that area. No response. But a commercial pilot heading in the same direction had heard my call. He continued on to Flores and reported a possible aircraft down in the jungles.

As the weather cleared up, he took off from Flores to search for us *somewhere down there*. To his great surprise he spotted us all standing by the plane on the airstrip at Sayaxche. He landed. I paid the farmer who lives next to the strip to keep his eyes on the plane until we could return and repair it. The commercial pilot loaded us aboard and took us back to Guatemala City. A God-sent hero!

I did a mental assessment, then borrowed a replacement cylinder from a pilot in Guatemala City. A friend flew me out to the abandoned plane. He and I changed that cylinder out in the hot, humid jungle, with no shade, no extra equipment--terrible working conditions. We cranked her up and I flew my plane back to the city, at a very high altitude on a clear day.

I hadn't realized that the engine in my plane had cylinders installed which were *not* stamped with an "H" denoting heavy-duty. This plane's cylinders were standard ones which would not hold up nearly as long.

Sure enough, we found that the head had separated from the body of the number five cylinder, causing oil to be pumped out of a huge crack onto the hot exhaust. That explained the smoke in the cabin. If I hadn't cut the power when I did, the head would have separated completely, destroying the entire engine.

Since that replacement cylinder had been borrowed from another pilot, when our new cylinder arrived from the states, we had to make the change-over again. At least this time we could do the work in a hangar at Guatemala City.

After this incident, I made a little placard which I placed under the gas gauges on the passenger side of the plane: "THIS ENGINE MAY FAIL, BUT JESUS NEVER FAILS!" I mentally added "*AMEN*!"

ANIMALS and AIRSTRIPS

That day after Christmas found us relaxed, still in a holiday mood. The calm was shattered by a call requesting an emergency flight to San Andres. Two drunken men had been badly wounded in a machete fight. Someone from a neighboring town was calling for help.

The airstrip at San Andres was one we had built for the Mennonites. Though a good airstrip, the farmer's cattle loved wandering over to graze on its tall grass, making it rather dangerous. We always had to check things out with a pre-landing pass. If occupied by animals, chasing them off required several low passes, consuming extra gas and time. After much discussion with the local farmers, we had finally built a fence around the airstrip. But at times, the fence would be surreptitiously cut. Thus we were always rather tense coming in, never knowing what we might find.

Animals or no, I had to answer this emergency call. I hurried off to the airport, got the plane, filed a flight plan and took off in the usual good weather of our dry season. Arriving, I flew over low to *do a visual* of the fence and check for cattle or animals on the airstrip. This wasn't easy since, without cattle regularly grazing on the field, the grass had grown about a foot tall, easily hiding a small cow or calf.

I did notice several cows under a tree next to the fence, but all were safely on the far side of the fence. Satisfied, I made the approach, cleared the fence and planted the main gear firmly on the ground. The tail wheel wasn't yet down when I spotted a calf *inside* the fence. I hadn't seen him since he was standing close to his mama who was outside the fence. But this calf was definitely on the airstrip side of the fence. Right then, the airplane noise frightened him. Alas, the only way he could run was toward the airstrip--in front of me!

Instinctively, I braked. Uh oh, a tad too hard! Tail in the air, the plane flipped over on its back, landing upside down amid the high grass. Thankfully, my shoulder harness held me. When I undid the seatbelt, I fell on my head but was able to crawl out to survey the damage. I wasn't hurt, but the plane was-- bent propeller blade and one wing with a small dent. Not too bad. As I breathed a sigh of relief, that pesky calf just stood there looking at me!

Well, I wouldn't be going home that night, for sure. How could I contact Chiqui to tell her I was okay? The village was only about a mile away, but it had no telephone service, just a telegraph operator who, during holidays, was nowhere to be found. We hadn't yet installed our HF radios and, with no cell phones in those days, I was completely incommunicado. Nothing to do but wait.

As evening fell, the Christian brothers from the village arrived, as I knew they would. They brought me food, water and a mattress to sleep on. We prayed together and they left. I prepared for the night—one of the worst I have known in my life.

Why so bad, since I was safe? Well, I was tortured by terrible feelings of *if only*. If only I had checked more carefully for cattle. If only I hadn't over-reacted and over-braked. If only I wasn't flying my brand-new plane.

That same 'If Only' theme touches so many of us after an accident or a tragedy in our lives. We can drive ourselves into great depression dwelling on it. I didn't sleep very well that night, out there under the stars on that mattress, with my brand-new, unpaid-for airplane in bad shape. And what about those men injured by machetes still waiting for me?

In the meantime, back in Guatemala City, Chiqui knew that I was supposed to be back by at least three o'clock. At five o'clock I hadn't shown up. She realized I wasn't coming home, but had no idea whether I was dead or alive. Of course, she had a rough night ahead of her, just as she had so many times over the past thirty-five years, times when I wasn't able to get back because of weather or mechanical problems. Now she was going through that torment again. Though she had a strong faith, this type of situation was always a challenge for her.

She called to see if any one at Aeronautica had heard anything on radio. Had I reported in? "Nobody has reported in." Then she called the Aeroclub, but they had heard nothing. In desperation she called the Air Force to report a missing airplane and request a search. She was told, "Well, this being holidays, it's hard to get anything going. We could probably search for him, but not until tomorrow. There isn't much daylight left now."

About seven o'clock that evening a final option occurred to her. She called a missionary friend of mine who happened to be in Guatemala at the time with a twin engine aircraft. Chiqui told him what had happened. "Well, it's so dark it would be impossible to see anything now. But I'll sure be out there with the first rays of the sun in the morning." Bless his heart, he certainly was. Gathering up Chiqui, he went out at five-thirty in the morning, cranked up his engine and they took off for San Andres. I heard the airplane at sunrise. To let them know I was fine, I stood by the plane waving furiously as he circled over the landing strip.

Of course, with my wrecked plane on the airstrip, they couldn't land there. But about ten miles away, in this same valley, lay an airstrip adequate for landing his twin engine airplane. He flew there and let Chiqui out. Immediately, he took off again for the city to notify Civil Aeronáutica of our location and request a helicopter to bring us out. Couageously, Chiqui hitched a ride to San Andres in the bed of a pickup truck amid the cargo, a cramped and jolting ride. But she was thankful she'd soon be with me.

About noon, a helicopter arrived with the official inspector of accidents. He carefully checked the airplane, noting all the accident details. By the time he had finished, quite a crowd had gathered. We enlisted some of the men to turn the plane back over onto its wheels. The damage was not that great but it wouldn't be flying. Some men helped me push the plane into the nearby hanger the Mennonites from the village had built.

Chiqui and I flew back in the helicopter to Guatemala City. What a wonderful feeling to be safely home with my family! And the plane was safe. There were sad feelings, too. Although insured for damages, my new airplane wasn't paid for.

To get it repaired, we first had to figure out how to get it out of San Andres. With the only road in that valley barely passable in the dry season, we were so thankful that it *was* the dry season. But still, the road was just a path across the mountains, full of holes and ruts, crossing streams with no bridges. A rough trek.

I hired a truck, a driver and a couple of guys I felt were up to the task of hauling the plane back to the city. The next day I flew back out with a missionary friend in his plane. He and I removed the plane wings, ready to fit the body of the plane into the back of the truck. When the truck arrived, with the help of about a dozen men, we rolled the plane up on the truck bed. The two detached wings fit in on each side of the plane. We secured all. My friend flew back to the city. I joined the driver for the return trip, determined to leave my troubling 'If Only' thoughts behind in San Andres.

We hauled the crippled plane to the Cessna dealer, unloading it in their hangar. The dealership began the repair work. In 'only' four months it was repaired. That lengthy delay arose from a major, unanticipated issue. The company who manufactures the engine had a rigid safety stipulation. If a sudden stoppage of one of their motors occurs for *any* reason, the entire engine must be disassembled so the crank shaft could be examined for cracks. Yes, the whole engine— the crank shaft is the back-bone of the engine.

94

I could do that myself, so I made arrangements at the Cessna dealership to use a part of their service area to completely dismantle the engine. I removed the crankshaft. It passed inspection. Then, reversing that long process, I completely rebuilt the motor. I managed this huge job with the help of some of the dealership mechanics who kindly gave me a hand.

All those months I was without my airplane. Fortunately, a business man I knew had a Cessna 182 and loaned it to me, so I could still fly missions. The plane wasn't a 185, but it would do.

Eventually, with the rebuilt engine and the wings and new tail re-attached, my 185 was ready to go again. It was basically in good shape. I continued to fly that Cessna 185 for many, many years. In fact, when the engine was nearing the time for an overhaul (2700 hours in those days), we ordered a new engine from the factory. I had it shipped to my brother's place in Texas. When it arrived, I flew up to Texas, took the old engine out and put the new engine in. I managed to get it all squared away in a short time. I did a test run flying around the airstrip in Texas to make sure that everything was working properly. Finally satisfied with her, I took off, flew down to Brownsville, on down to Vera Cruz and across to Guatemala. She performed perfectly. And we met up with no animals on runways.

AGITATED AMBASSADOR

That morning began with a most unusual phone call. It was from the office of the United States Embassy. I didn't remember ever hearing that anyone had been called by that esteemed agency unless someone was in big trouble.

This was the Ambassador's secretary on the line. She began with general inquiries about my flying knowledge of Guatemala's more remote regions. That led to a question about the possibility of my flying the Ambassador to a strip located in the eastern part of the country. It was obviously a very special request. After recovering from the surprise, I informed her that, yes, I did know the airstrip in question. And, yes, I could take him there.

But I puzzled at the request. When the Ambassador from the United States of America needed to go somewhere, all he had to do was to contact the Guatemalan Air Force and they would provide helicopters. I continued to be perplexed about why I was called for this flight—possibly because he wanted to go incognito to a difficult spot. Well, that was not *my* concern. So I made arrangements with the secretary for the date and the hour of the flight. My instructions to them were to meet me at the gas pumps at the Aeroclub.

Meanwhile, I needed to carefully calculate the amount of gas required for that trip. Ordinarily, I never filled my gas tanks to capacity. I might, if I were planning a long trip or ferrying gas to one of our bases out in the mountains. On those occasions (and this one) I would have to take many factors into consideration: estimated distance, weather and wind direction, weight of the passengers and luggage, flying time, including a small reserve. Finally, the length and condition of the airstrip--hard surface, grass, potholes or other obstacles. Neglecting to consider even a single factor could be fatal. I would take the calculated amount of gasoline.

Filling with the correct amount of gas was a challenge, since the electrical gas gauges on these aircraft are notably unreliable. Our sister mission organization MAF had developed a unique way to measure the exact amount of gas onboard a Cessna 180 or 185. These planes are *tail-draggers*, sitting on the ground at an angle. MAF had designed a piece of aluminum to fit into these gas tanks, with marks to indicate different quantities of gas. I could climb up on the wing, insert this little piece of aluminum into the tank and get an accurate reading of just how much gasoline was onboard. Using this method, in all my years of flying I had never run out of fuel.

On the designated day I waited at the pumps. Right on time, two black limousines pulled up. The Ambassador greeted me and presented the two other passengers. Even though dressed as civilians, it was obvious that they were Marines--crew cuts, ram-rod straight, no nonsense in their demeanor. Both were carrying satchels. I couldn't examine the contents of their bags, so I had to estimate their weights by picking them up. It was evident they were not carrying potato chips and sandwiches! I didn't inquire as to what was in them. I added those weights to my other calculations and put in fuel for the trip.

Our destination was about thirty-five minutes of air time, but definitely not a straight-shot. We had to climb to 10,000 feet to clear the mountains, then drop sharply down into a valley. The airstrip sat at about the 3,000 foot elevation.

On landing, several military vehicles and some local dignitaries welcomed the Ambassador. The Ambassador told me they should not be much longer than a couple of hours. Off they drove to a destination unknown to me. They had given no indication that I was welcome to join them, so I remained at the airstrip, alone except for a couple of soldiers who simply stood around. I wondered if the mission was so top-secret and dangerous that I needed to stay with the guards to keep an eye on the plane. I never did find out what it was all about.

After lunch, the cadre returned. I re-seated my passengers, the Ambassador in the front with me and the two Marines in the back. We taxied to the end of the strip, checked everything out and away we went, clearing the tall trees with no problem. At this point, the flight from this particular airstrip always got exciting. The strip runs parallel to the mountains which rise steeply from 3,000 feet to about 10,000 feet. I had two 'official' options. One was to continue straight on, gaining enough altitude to fly over the mountains, then turn toward Guatemala City. Or I could circle right back over the airstrip, gaining the necessary altitude on that loop. Both options would take longer and burn more gasoline than our current weight restrictions would allow.

Instead, I opted for the way I had always done it. Since I knew the terrain, I turned left into a canyon wedged between the mountains. I was flying just above the trees while climbing at a steep angle. This canyon leads safely up and out on top. I knew this, but my passengers didn't.

Soon I noticed the Ambassador getting very nervous, very agitated about something. I assumed it was the steep climb barely above the trees. But soon he couldn't stand it any longer, grabbed my arm and nervously pointed to the electric gas gauges. At this angle they were showing EMPTY! Shakily he asked, "Do we have enough gas?" I nodded, "Yes, we have enough gas." I explained the unreliability of these gauges, also how I had personally dip-checked the tanks. Just then he noticed the little sign that I had stuck under the gas gauges: "THIS ENGINE MAY FAIL...BUT JESUS NEVER FAILS." "Is that true?" I nodded. He relaxed *slightly*.

Upon arrival in Guatemala City, I told him my story of how the Lord had miraculously saved our lives when the engine had failed. (May Day! May Day!) He listened very intently, just shaking his head. I never saw him again, but I prayed that he got the 'Jesus' part of that message!

JOLTED AWAKE

Chiqui was shouting, "Earthquake!" Jolted awake at three a.m., I felt our apartment reeling and rocking. My first thought was of our girls. I tried to run down the hallway to their room but could hardly stay upright. I was being thrown from wall to wall. In my wildest imagination, I could never have imagined a cement floor moving like liquid waves of an ocean, up and down, rolling. Staggering into the girls' room, I grabbed a mattress with my girl still on top, threw her and the mattress on top of her sister, then fell on top of them, praying to protect my precious girls.

I turned my head to look out the window. The trees were waving back and forth in the most surrealistic fashion you could ever imagine. Power lines were snapping all over the city with flashes of electricity lighting the night sky. Otherwise there was no electricity in the whole city; everything was dark and dead silent.

As soon as the earthquake began to subside, Chiqui and I grabbed some clothes and the girls, intent on getting out as quickly as possible. Broken glass was strewn everywhere. Pictures had fallen off the walls. All the dishes were on the floor. The refrigerator had come open, with food spilled all over the floor. Weaving through, we made it out without cutting our feet. We were headed to where our van was parked. In those years of traveling for weekend preaching, we had a van in which I had built a bed for sleeping. Now we four made it safely to the van and slept there until dawn.

I arose just at dawn, checked the building to make sure our neighbors were all okay. The apartment building had been constructed with a cement roof, cement floors and cement walls, built to withstand earthquakes. It did sustain a few superficial cracks, but nothing serious. How it stood up, I'll never know. We were among Guatemala's most fortunate.

[1]The 7.5 earthquake of February 4, 1976, was one of the strongest of many to hit Guatemala. Twenty three thousand people were killed, about a million left homeless, all in about a minute and a half that early morning. The streets were deserted as I looked around our neighborhood. I saw several buildings with great gaping holes in them, where parts of the walls had collapsed. Some buildings were totally down.

As the sun was just coming up, I rode my bike to the airport and pulled out the airplane. I wanted to fly around to see the extent of the damage. Of course, all tower communication had been disrupted. No one was directing planes—if there *had* been planes. There weren't. There was no evidence that anyone was at the airport. I was the first airplane to take off that morning.

As I flew over the city, headed out to villages where missionary friends lived, I could still see dust coming up from several areas where homes and buildings had collapsed. I flew toward the fault line, to

---

[1] National Geospatial-Intelligence Agency

my friend Bill's village of Joyabaj. Looking down, my fears were confirmed--that village of adobe buildings was now mostly flat rubble. There were maybe one or two buildings left standing in the entire village. I flew on to assess damage at some other villages. I found the same sad situation.

Turning back, I landed at Joyabaj. Bill heard the plane land and came running to the airstrip. His whole family had survived, miraculously. He was covered with adobe dust, just two white streaks down his face from his tears. He was in shock. "We need help, badly!" I had nothing but prayers to offer, so flew back to Guatemala City to see what help I could organize from there.

Flying in, I could see people were beginning to move about. Organized search and rescue needed to begin as soon as possible. Many people would still be trapped in their houses, many thousands more injured. As I landed, some bomberos (firemen) asked me where I had come from, wanting to get some idea of the extent of the damage. Since there was no electricity, no telephones, they'd had no reports. I described where I had been and filled them in about what I had seen. They hustled me downtown to the government radio station TGW, the only radio station operating at that time, powered now by a generator. I was put on the air to give a firsthand report of the damage to people with battery radios.

Then I went back home to check on my family. Chiqui had gotten our portable stove out. There in our garden she had set up house-keeping. She had what food she could salvage from the refrigerator and we had water to drink. The girls thought this was great fun, getting to sleep in the van, play and eat breakfast outside. We would be 'camping out' in the garden and van for some time. We did not feel safe returning to our apartment.

In fact, it would be several months before we could bring ourselves to sleep in the building. The trauma of that night just wouldn't go away. And because after-shocks continued for about two weeks, you never knew when another shaking might hit—or if it might be another 'Big One'. All of a sudden things would start rattling, shaking, the buildings quivering again. It was terribly hard on everyone's nerves.

After checking on the family, I ate some breakfast, then went back to the airport to see what I could do. It was buzzing with activity now. The Air Force was organizing, trying to figure out how to deal with this tragedy. They knew it would involve complex air operations, since all the main roads were blocked by many of the 10,000 landslides. It was impossible to travel outside the city except towards the less-damaged south coast.

The Aeroclub to which I belonged became the center of logistics to get survival supplies, medicines, medical supplies, doctors and people out to key areas. Their plan of action was to form three squadrons of twelve civilian pilots, each with a flight leader. They selected only pilots who had experience flying in some of the more remote areas. I was chosen as one of them.

That plan put us under the direction of our squadron leader. He would receive requests for flights, get the location, then call one of his squadron pilots to make the flight. Each day, all day, we lined up at the airport, ready to respond at a moment's notice. People carried in supplies, other volunteers loaded the planes.

Airplanes were already flying in from many countries to help. The Guatemala City airport was severely taxed. All day long, huge cargo airliners, one after another, were landing, unloading, refueling and taking off again. Massive quantities of goods were pouring into Guatemala. The USA had already flown down a couple of big C-5 Galaxy planes. One flew in with a complete hospital onboard--operating room, ambulances, doctors, nurses, medicines, blankets and food.

To coordinate this massive operation safely, the USAF flew in by helicopter jeeps equipped as portable control towers. With these, the US military personnel became our air controllers. It certainly did need controlling, with planes circling above, planes lined up on the airfield. The GIs directed all this traffic, with us reporting to them for take-off and landing instructions, just like at any major airport control tower. They were doing a superbly professional job.

Our civilian Aeroclub planes parked at the gas pumps, where we sat until our squadron leader called, "Okay, Don, you're going to such and such a place with this load." We'd fly to that destination and back, park back by the gas pumps where we refueled at no charge. Then another call, "You're going to this other place. You got this load."

Volunteers sorted goods in the hangars by the Aeroclub. What a challenge for them to sort medicines, blankets, food, plumbing supplies, saws, hammers and tools to dig out those trapped in the rubble. They went through, identified and tried to make certain the right supplies got loaded on the right plane.

For us civilian pilots, it was exciting. Sometimes we'd take off two at a time on the runway, something regulations certainly had never allowed before. But this was an urgent military operation. In another 'never before' we used three stretches of highway as landing strips! Not only was this now allowed, it was essential in order to move all the planes needed for the recovery mission. At any rate, no vehicles could use those highways—they were blocked by debris to the north, east and west. The segments of highway selected were runway-straight, with no obstacles, so the military declared these as official airstrips.

Since the roads were not wide, we formed up single file on our assigned stretch of highway. Planes stacked up one behind the other while unloading wounded people, then were reloaded with whatever needed to be flown out. When you got to the front of the line, you'd take off with supplies to places most pilots had never flown—to wherever they had been requested. After each 'Special Delivery' we flew back to the Capital.

So my squadron leader gave me my destination and the GIs directed my take-off and landings on various ones of those three highways. We flew that way every day, all day, with food and drinks brought in for the pilots in abundance by thoughtful people.

Another sort of flying duty was not in the least exciting. At all times one pilot had to fly a continuous circular pattern at 10,000 feet to relay messages via VHF radio. That was the only way to receive calls from the disaster areas requesting urgently needed items. The circulating pilot would then call into the Aeroclub to assure that those items were loaded and sent out immediately. When a pilot was assigned to this duty, he groaned. It was essential, but boring, to fly in that circle for our rotating (pun intended) assignment of a couple hours at a time.

Other than that duty, something different or exciting was always occurring. I remember one day standing on the highway at Chimaltenango talking to the other pilots as our planes were being unloaded. All of a sudden I heard a loud explosion, like dynamite or a bomb going off. As we looked around, the road where all our planes were sitting began to weave just like a snake, causing our planes to begin shaking. We could see the shock rolling towards us, coming on like waves of the ocean. When it reached us, we could hardly stand. And that was a *mere* after-shock!

Another day I was assigned to fly out a load of supplies, landing on one of the highways. I was also carrying a special passenger, one of the finest photographers from the National Geographic Society. He'd been sent to capture the recovery operations going on in Guatemala. This particular highway was quite narrow, but I landed us safely. As I waited my turn to take off again, he and I were standing under the wing talking. Like any professional photographer, he had camera in hand, ready for action. His camera, rare in those days, was one which would take a sequence of pictures by just holding down the shutter.

As we chatted, we observed a plane approaching our narrow road, trying to land in a brisk crosswind. It became evident he was not an experienced pilot. He began to weave with the winds whipping around him. As he touched down, one of his wheels dropped off the pavement onto a bit of a shoulder. Then he lost it. The plane swerved straight toward a pickup truck, loaded ready to take supplies out to villages. A young man was resting in the back of that truck. As the airplane headed right for him, he looked up, saw the plane and jumped out, just as the airplane hit the back end of that pickup.

The Geographic magazine photographer 'just happened' to be taking a picture sequence of the landing. Thus he had captured a picture of the young man leaping out of the pickup the moment the airplane hit. That photo won a first prize for the year. It was a classic, worth a lot of money. Note: No one was hurt.

On another occasion, I was with a group of pilots sitting in our Ready Room, awaiting a flying assignment. Two Guatemalan Air Force helicopter pilots came rushing in with an urgent request: "We have a load of medicine, urgently needed to take to a place we do not know where it is. Does anybody here know where the village of Castanas is?" Well, I had preached in that little village in the middle of nowhere. I was the only one who knew where it was.

My squadron leader gave me permission to accompany these two pilots to show them the way. I climbed into that huge Guatemalan Airforce Huey helicopter. Then I, a gringo civilian pilot, proceeded to show the Big Guys where Castanas was. As we landed in a corn field, the pastor at that church was on hand to coordinate the mission. He was really surprised to see me sitting in a big military helicopter! We chatted a moment. He urged us to continue to pray for his little earthquake-damaged village.

Day after day for nearly a month we flew search and rescue missions over the affected areas. We observed badly damaged scenic areas, such as whole sides of mountains split in two. One slide dammed up a little creek. Years later it had formed a beautiful little lake. Other times we'd be flying along when, all of a sudden, great big clouds of dust roiled up off unstable mountains, evidence of another strong after-shock.

A different sort of incredible sight was seeing how the world responded to Guatemala's earthquake. The United States government and the American people did much of it. Guatemalans observed how evangelical Christians from all over the USA volunteered, helping build houses, repairing churches. They were impressed that people came to help from the States for months after the earthquake.

It was then that the phenomenal growth of the evangelical church in Guatemala began, in response to the tremendous outpouring of love by Christians. The people of Guatemala were overwhelmed, saying, "We cannot believe these Christians, their dedication and their love for us, coming here to build these villages." It was a great testimony for all of Guatemala.

The earthquake had sent people out screaming in the streets. In many villages, they told us later, people were crying out to God, repenting of sin. From a country with few evangelicals, it became one of the largest evangelical communities in all of Latin America. Thus Guatemala, at the end of 1976, began transforming into a country with a strong leadership position among Latin American countries.

Not only did the 1976 earthquake awaken Chiqui and me from our sleep, it had shaken Guatemalans from their spiritual sleep.

ENTERPRISING ELAM

The adage "Never judge a man by first appearances" was never truer than in this case. My first impression was that he looked rather different from most of the people in the Lancaster, PA, area—quite short and stocky, with blonde hair.

I had just finished preaching an evening service when he came up with his wife and children. Introducing himself as Elam Stoltfus, he related that he and his family had left the Amish religion, been gloriously converted and were now assisting in an evangelical church.

Then the conversation took an unusual twist. Recently he had felt God calling him specifically to Guatemala. He'd seen a newspaper notice that missionaries from Guatemala were speaking at tonight's service. He explained that he and his family wanted to go to some remote area where no one else had gone. Did I know if there were areas like that in Guatemala? I described the northern region that was all jungle, no roads, no conveniences, just small remote villages.

He seemed pleased with that information, thanking me profusely before leaving. I shook my head. It seemed a rather risky scheme for an unsophisticated man to haul his young family off to such a very remote area. Well, probably he planned to form a team of other mission-minded families from Lancaster.

Some time later, back in Guatemala, Elam appeared at our apartment door. He announced that he had come with his family to begin a ministry and wanted me to fly him out to look for a suitable place where he and his family could begin ministry. Despite my concerns, we made plans to do so.

Revving up my plane, we flew over the northern region, following the Passion River. We spotted some scattered villages just where the river made a 180 degree turn. He thought the surrounding heavily-forested area looked promising. A mission tucked in that 180 turn, with river on three sides, would give good river travel access and some measure of protection.

Then he surprised me by saying that he wasn't ready to fly back to the city. He wanted to boat down the river to check things out. I explained that the closest landing strip was in Sayache, followed by a two hour trip down-river by powered launch to the site we'd spotted. I wasn't sure it would be wise. He had never been in any jungle areas before. No, he was determined to see if that land was available. So I dropped him off at the Sayache airstrip, wished him God's blessings and agreed to pick him up a few days later.

During those few days he had already purchased land at that bend in the river. Was that an early clue to his enterprising nature? His plan was to return with his family and a houseboat on a trailer, then start clearing the land. It did not bother him in the least that there was no electricity or drinking water nearby. Growing up in the Amish culture, all that had been a normal part of his life.

So back he went to Pennsylvania, then pulled a houseboat all the way through Mexico, Belize and over bumpy Guatemalan dirt roads to the Passion River. He slid his houseboat into the river, with his family, their goods and jungle-clearing supplies, floating them downstream to his new home-site. I could see I would be busy flying supplies back and forth to Sayache for some time.

On one occasion he asked me to come and help him plan ahead for an airstrip on his property. As we sat in his houseboat drinking some lemonade, I was curious and asked him where he got his water. "From the river." He had run a pipe from the houseboat out to the middle of the river where it rested on the bottom. "Well yes, of course, we boil it."

The Amish community had given him a portable sawmill, so he began using his special talents working with wood. Beautiful hardwood trees on his property provided plenty of material. With his two boys, he built a church and a small clinic. Last on the list was a home for the family. Everything was made of the finest mahogany wood, even the pews in that small jungle church!

Elam and his wife began to minister to basic medical needs in the little clinic they had built. Neither had any first aid training but they did what they could. Living far out in the jungles, anything is better than nothing. People showed up with a wide range of medical problems. Most were manageable.

One day a man came with severe pain in his side. Elam could tell that the situation was very serious. He got on his ham radio and began to broadcast for a doctor somewhere in the world who could give him some advice. He located a willing doctor in the USA. From Elam's descriptions, the doctor diagnosed a severe case of appendicitis. So what was Elam to do? The doctor said the man needed surgery as soon as possible or he would die. Elam explained that getting him to a hospital from their remote location was totally out of the question. The situation obviously called for drastic measures. Enter Enterprising Elam.

Unbelievably, that doctor led Elam and his wife, step-by-step, through performing an appendectomy! He began with how to apply anesthesia and where to make the incision. After that, Elam was back-and-forth to his radio getting further instructions, returning each time to continue the operation. When they had the abdomen open, he had no idea where or what the appendix looked like. Back to his radio to ask the doctor how to find it amid all that bloody tissue. Amazingly, Elam was able to locate the appendix and remove it. Even more amazing, the man survived the ordeal, making a total recovery. Truly the guiding hand of God.

Eventually we laid out an airstrip, starting at the river for a good approach, with high trees at the other end. Elam and his sons cleared the strip with the help of men from the villages, using nothing but basic tools and hard manual labor. Removing the stumps of these huge trees without a tractor was extremely time-consuming. People from villages in the area came to help the family in many ways.

Elam let me know when the airstrip was ready, I told him the day and hour I would fly in to inaugurate the new strip. Everyone from the nearby village came out for this great occasion. I circled a few times, looking it over very carefully before deciding to land. The men had done their best, clearing out the stumps and leveling the holes. But for a small airplane, it was still extremely rough. I bounced like crazy, nearly jolting my teeth out, but made it in. After the celebration, I gave them instructions on how to level every bump, which they did. It turned out to be an excellent airstrip which I used frequently.

Now began the most wonderful, blessed time for many years. Oh, what a joy to be able to serve such wonderful servants of the Lord, the finest missionary family I ever knew. And how many varied experiences we had on that airstrip.

One that stands out is when Elam decided to introduce honey bees to the villagers. I flew out a plane-load of honey bees in little boxes with screen on three sides and some water. During the flight I noticed several bees out of their boxes. What if they stung me? (The flight would have been much less stressful had I known that bees can't fly above 10,000 feet.) All went well-- until I started down into the jungle. But, even with those bees buzzing angrily all around my head, I managed to land without getting stung. One of the boys unloading the boxes didn't fare so well.

Among later projects, an Amish organization gave Elam two mules. They were shipped down, hauled by cart to Sayache, then walked to the mission. He loaned them out to help people clear their land. Some fine dairy cows from another Amish organization were shipped down. I flew out special containers with frozen semen. He had the cows artificially inseminated, building up a good herd. Then he shared his cattle so others could build up herds to produce dairy products.

On another occasion, I was at home with no flights planned. I was really enjoying a day with the family when the phone rang. It was long distance from Minnesota, a medical doctor. He explained that he had been listening to his ham radio when he heard an emergency call from a missionary in the jungles of northern Guatemala. He said the missionary had nearly severed his thumb in an accident with his hand-saw. The missionary was seeking advice over the ham radio. The doctor told him if he could get to a hospital soon, his thumb could possibly be saved.

He said the man's name was Elam! He had asked the doctor to call me in Guatemala and see if I could fly him to the city for surgery. Thanking the doctor, I immediately went to the hangar, got the plane out, filed my flight plan and took off for the hour flight to Elam's place. Fortunately the weather was good, so it was not a difficult flight.

When I arrived, Elam and his wife were waiting for me, Elam's thumb wrapped in a thick bandage. I got them in the plane, we took off to Guatemala City where I took him to a hospital. The surgeons saved his thumb. It was a little stiff but he was able to use it effectively for the rest of his life.

When Elam's oldest son, Virgil, turned sixteen, they sent him to the States where he learned to fly an airplane. They first bought an Ultralight aircraft. With it, Virgil could make the short flight to the area's main airport for supplies and emergencies. Later on they were able to acquire a single engine bush plane which they used effectively for many years.

Then tragedy struck Elam's beautiful little paradise of Buenas Nuevas (Good News). For years the Communist insurgence had been very active in that area, trying to convert people to Communism. The Communists eventually realized that the main impediment to their goal was Elam. Everyone knew the Stoltfus family ministry and were impressed with their beautiful example of brotherly love.

The Communist leaders decided to send a gang to eliminate that impediment. Their instructions were to burn everything to the ground--tractor, airplane and all buildings on the mission compound. Then to give Elam and his family twenty-four hours to leave the country.

But they were to kill Virgil. Why kill Virgil? Virgil was very outgoing and took a strong stand for the Lord. Everybody loved Virgil. Since he was only in his twenties, he would be a menace to the Communist agenda for years.

One night a gang of Communists charged in at midnight. They roused everyone, let them get a few belongings to load in their boat. Virgil was taken prisoner. As Elam, Barbara and their other children got into their boat, flames illuminated that dark night. The insurgents gathered up electronics, medicine and other valuable stuff, filling two boats. They took off, Virgil and his two guards with them, leaving only ashes behind.

Down the river the gang went, Virgil still in tow. After about an hour they turned off into a creek, finally coming to a little landing where the insurgents had their camp. The men left Virgil at the river with two guards. The guards told Virgil to sit there quietly while they unloaded the stuff. One of the guards left his AK 47 in the boat. Virgil noticed the weapon, so he quietly picked it up and put it in his lap.

When one of the men returned for another load, Virgil put the barrel of the gun up to the man's head and said quietly, "Don't make a move or I'll blow your head off." The man begin to shake violently and cry out for mercy. The other arrived and immediately raised his hands and both of them cried "Please don't kill us!" Virgil told me later that he hadn't even known where the trigger was or if the safety was on or off. But the men didn't know that. He had the drop on them.

Next Virgil looked at them and said, "You guys came here to destroy and kill. My family and I came here to minister to these people, to help them. We have not come to kill anybody." He handed the weapon back to them and sat quietly looking at them. They were stunned. Why hadn't Virgil killed them? What they saw now was a man of remarkable courage. The man put down the AK 47. Yes, they had instructions to kill Virgil, but they could not do it. In the next days they began to treat him with great kindness.

After a few days one of the Communist officials came back through. He was surprised to see that Virgil was still alive. Very angry, he shouted, "KILL HIM, KILL HIM!" He left, saying he would return the next day to make sure they had followed his orders. The captors said to Virgil, "We do not want to harm you, but if we don't, we will be killed." Still, they couldn't bring themselves to do it. So they chained him to a tree, hoping it might be easier to kill him under the dark of night. They dozed.

Late in the night they woke, hearing loud noises in the jungle. About a hundred men came storming through the jungle from nearby villages where Virgil had ministered for many years. They wielded big knives and announced to the two guards, "We have come to get Virgil. We will take him with us. You have machine guns and we only have machetes. You will probably kill a lot of us, but you two *will* be killed. So give us Virgil now, and we will leave." The men released him and the villagers left safely with Virgil.

The Stoltfus ministry never recovered from that night of destruction. Elam and his wife returned to the states. Virgil married a lady from the USA and they live in Sayache, not far from the burned mission site. Elam went to his heavenly reward a few years ago. His wife, Barbara, is still in ministry work and occasionally visits Guatemala.

A humorous footnote to the sad ending: Over my many years of ministry together with Elam, whenever I flew to the Stoltfus mission, several outboard motors awaited repair. Enterprising Elam's time and interests apparently didn't include motorboat engine repair

PEDRITO'S PECULIAR GARDEN

Guatemala's rugged mountain ridges are spectacularly beautiful, but presented significant challenges to Mennonite missionaries working in the central highlands. The group obviously realized their work could be greatly aided by our plane services but they had no landing strips and a serious shortage of level land for constructing any.

They asked me to help in the search for any areas they might use for landing strips. From the air I saw a couple of places where it looked as if small planes could possibly land. When we spotted a good prospect, I landed in a farmer's field and the missionary negotiated with the farmer for permission to use his field for a landing strip. They rented a narrow strip down the middle of his field, so the farmer could still plant and harvest corn.

With some work, a short landing strip was eked out there and at two other highland locations that I had spotted. All permits were properly applied for and authorized by Aeronautics, so flights began. Air services were valuable in expanding the mission work and serving those communities.

A few years later the civil war reared its ugly head in the central highlands. It was so bad that the government labeled it an official "war zone." For me, that meant "no-fly zone." I was still permitted to fly in other areas, so I could tune into Air Force frequencies. I heard talk about dropping bombs and deciding where to strafe with machine guns and rockets. Distressing to hear, but far worse for the pastors and churches I had come to know and love in those war areas.

One day the mayor and some men from one of the villages appeared at my door with an urgent request to fly them home to their village. Sadly, I had to inform them that it was impossible. Their area had been declared off-limits to all civilian aviation activities. Besides, it was just too dangerous. As they went out the door, I added, "The only way would be for you to obtain written permission from the head of the Air Force." Of course, I knew it would be impossible for them to get that permission, so why had I even said that?

The next day they returned--with a signed document by the commanding officer of the Air Force! It granted me permission to make one flight, on a specified day and time slot. That day, with written permission firmly in my hand, we flew out of Guatemala City, heading for the village. The script running continuously through my brain was, *I sure hope they informed everyone in this area about our flight.* I could picture myself being shot down in flames, clutching my written permission and yelling, "Hey, wait guys! My permission is right here!"

That made for tense flying, but we landed in the village with no difficulty. My passengers were certainly happy to be safely home. As I prepared for takeoff, the pastor walked up. Could I take a patient to the hospital for a checkup in a neighboring town? Pedrito, his head swathed in bandages, followed, so we helped him climb into the plane. As we took off, I inquired about what had happened to him. He replied, "Me pegaron." (They shot me.) Here is his story, with a truly amazing twist at the very end:

Pedrito was a young Indian man from a very rural area. He didn't have much education, but was a faithful follower of the Lord. He lived alone in a small house about a mile from the village. One day two men charged into his house with a weapon, demanding he give them money, food or whatever. Pedrito didn't have much money, so they grabbed several of his chickens.

As they were leaving, one of them spied his Bible on the table. "He is a Christian! Let's kill him." They took him outside, pushed him up against the wall and backed up a few paces. One man aimed his weapon at Pedrito's head. Knowing this was the end, Pedrito prayed softly, not crying out for mercy, just praying to his Lord and waiting for the bullet.

But these men were used to seeing people crying out, sobbing and pleading "Don't kill me. Don't kill me." Pedrito's quiet response stunned the two men. The one with the weapon began to shake. The other kept yelling, "Shoot him! Shoot him!" So he fired both barrels of the old shotgun. He was shaking so badly that one shot hit the wall, the other scraped along one side of Pedrito's head, literally scalping that side. The force threw him against the wall where he fell to the ground.

Pedrito told me that his spirit came out of his body and ascended about twenty feet into the air, where he could look down and see himself lying on the ground. He heard the two men talking as he floated above them. One robber was saying, "Is he dead?" They became so nervous, they just ran off. Pedrito said his spirit came back down into his body and he regained consciousness. He managed to crawl into his house before he fainted.

At that week's evening prayer meeting, Pedrito wasn't there. He never missed a service, so when he didn't show up that evening, the others knew something must be wrong. The next day they walked out to his house and found him lying in a pool of blood. Picking him up, they carried him into the village where they treated him the best they could. It was obvious he needed more care, but how could they get him to a hospital? The only possible way was to carry him to the nearest dirt road. But that was seven miles over a mountain ridge in an area controlled by insurgents. If they were discovered, they would all be killed.

"Well, he is our Christian brother. We must do it." So a group of believers left on that very dangerous journey, carrying their brother in the Lord over the ridge. Wearily, they trudged to the road where they flagged down a pickup truck. Loading him in, they made it safely to the Christian Hospital in Quiche. There he was cared for expertly by the head doctor, Dr. DeLeon.

Dr. DeLeon later told me the incredible rest of the story. The two bandits had shot Pedrito with an ancient shotgun. They apparently didn't have the proper buckshot, so they had made their own, using small kernels of black beans. When Dr. DeLeon began cleaning up the wound on Pedrito's head, he discovered that the beans were beginning to sprout, buried in his scalp! He plucked them out and bandaged the wound. (Medical note: the serum in the open, raw tissue made an excellent culture medium—but not for long-term gardening.)

After Pedrito had told me his story, I inquired what his plans were for the future. He replied that he would remain in his village and continue in the work to which the Lord had called him--to be a faithful servant of his Master. He knew he would face dangerous times ahead, but his desire was to follow the Lord.

TEXAS TALES

This story isn't about me, although I am definitely a Texan. I do appear in this story, but in a supporting role. The leading role of Texan in this story is a man named Jim. I don't know all the details of his life, but I will let the cameras roll on this unique, unforgettable character.

After World War II there were many young airmen looking for jobs and/or adventures. Somehow Jim heard that down in Central America there was a great need for cropdusters. That sounded like an exciting adventure, so he took off in his plane for Central America. He found that, at that time, most of the good land in the south coast was dedicated to bananas, later on cotton. These two crops needed to be fumigated from the air so Jim found plenty of opportunities to earn money cropdusting independently.

Eventually he landed a permanent job on one of the largest farms, owned by one of the richest families in Guatemala. The man who hired Jim happened to have a daughter. You guessed it--they got married. Jim now became an important part of running the family's farming operations.

Over time, Jim noted that Guatemala was beginning to expand beyond agriculture. Several oil companies were showing interest in the northern part of Guatemala. The only way to get to that remote area was by air. Jim saw the need for a first-class air taxi service. Others were interested in this type of business

124

venture. But their goal was to make great sums of money in the shortest possible time, investing the least possible amount of money when acquiring airplanes and equipment which was not always very reliable.

So Jim formed his own company, Aviones Comerciales, to provide safe and reliable air taxi service. Unlike the others, Jim invested heavily in top quality airplanes. He purchased three Twin Otters, the top of the line of rugged aircraft made for rough airstrips. When this became known, naturally he obtained the most lucrative contracts.

I became acquainted with him when our family briefly attended the same church with Jim and his wife, strong evangelical Christians. He and I connected both as pilots and Texans. It mattered not that I was flying for a small missionary service, while he dealt with the Big Boys, the oil companies. We got along very well and I would stop by his office occasionally to visit. His office had windows opening up to their huge hangars. As he fixed coffee, he'd grumble if too many planes were in the hangar. "They're not making any money sitting in the hanger."

Though a successful business man, he still wanted to talk about things of the Lord. One day he surprised me by saying, "I want to hire you as a copilot for the company." Since I had my captain's bars, when I had some free time I went over to the operation and flew co-pilot on the Twin Otters

His motives to hire me as a copilot were two-fold. First was safety. Most pilots were not exactly the type you will find in church on Sunday morning. They came to work still under the influence of severe hangovers, wife problems, mistress problems, girlfriend battles and other sundry burdens--in no condition to fly, for sure. Jim knew that even just their reputation could potentially jeopardize the entire operation.

Secondly, Jim definitely had an interest in the souls of his pilots. With that in mind, he wanted me to fly with them as a safe and sober co-pilot, at the same time doing counseling. The beauty of this arrangement was that they did not look at me as a minister or missionary. To them, I was just another pilot. They were more willing to open up to me completely, freely telling me all the sordid details of their lives. A normal flight would be one hour or less, plenty of time to witness of God's message of love and life. Some began to get the message. We had some real conversions.

I was also finding it exciting being in on the burgeoning oil industry. One time we landed right next to a big rig belonging to Texaco. Our task was to pick up the crew and drop off the new, fresh crew. Loading up, I spotted a big heavy-set 'gringo' in a Stetson with boots. It took no stretch of imagination to know he was from Texas. This fella had the very important job as driller. He was carrying a plastic gallon container with him. I asked, in a good Texan drawl, "What 'cha got in that jug?" He looked at me with a big grin and said, "Texas tea." The well had come gushing in that morning at three a.m. He was carrying an oil sample back to Texaco's lab in Houston to check for quality.

To wind up this long Texas Tale, go back to how it began with Jim, our 'leading role' Texan who started crop dusting in Guatemala. He married well, managed the family business, founded the successful plane taxi service Aviones Comerciales, directed the gourmet food service for the booming oil camp--and hired me as a co-pilot. When Texas Jim passed away, his wife asked me to deliver a message at his funeral. What a blessed opportunity! Many very important people from the government, military, and the aviation community were in attendance. They heard the Gospel, not some Texas Tall Tale, but a True Tale, from a Texan. The rest of the story would be up to the Lord.

ADDED ATTRACTIONS

Another tremendous opportunity to evangelize came the long way around via Canada, oil in Guatemala and my brother-in-law, Luis Pérez. (Remember him, the one who brought his teenage sister named Chiqui to camp to go swimming?) Luis had graduated with high marks as an engineer from LeTourneau College in Texas. He and his roommate from Alberta, Canada, had talked about what they were going to do upon graduation. Luis' roommate invited him to Canada to work in the oil fields of northern Alberta. Luis decided to go, working in northern Alberta in the production end of the oil business. As an added bonus, he met his future wife.

Luis brought his new wife to Guatemala to meet and get acquainted with the Perez family. About that time, oil was discovered in Guatemala. This was a real boon for our mostly agricultural economy. While visiting, Luis made a life-changing discovery. The Guatemala oil industry needed to find a way to store and transport crude oil, but not one single Guatemalan had any experience in the production side of the industry. This is exactly what Luis had been doing in Canada for several years.

As you can imagine, Luis was hired on the spot. He was put in charge of transportation and storage facilities. Immediately, he was The Man! His first project was to build a nice long runway up there in Rubel Santo. The only way to get there was by air, so all supplies had to come the same way, on C-130 four-engine cargo planes.

Those were exciting times. Crews carved out from the jungle, not only the airfield, but an entire city for the workers. They brought in mobile buildings for all the personnel. Luis, of course, had the most luxurious one, quite comfortable with air conditioning. A dining hall was set up. All the food was catered in from the city, the express job of Jim, our 'leading role Texan'. What food! From the finest hotels in the city—it couldn't get any better. This was a real 'boom city' with new crews flown in every two weeks. WOW, was it a busy place!

I was flying around that area doing missionary work at small dirt air strips in the jungle. One day I decided to stop in and see how Luis was doing. Luis invited me to dinner. Man! Big steak, mashed potatoes, ice tea, ice cream, cake--all brought in from the finest restaurants in the city. Luis told the man in charge that I could eat there anytime! No charge! Needless to say, I did *happen* to stop by around noon quite frequently.

Luis' job had plopped him down right in the middle of a rowdy bunch of oil workers in the jungle, far away from everything. As a sincere Christian, Luis established guidelines. No women allowed! No liquor allowed! *Now* what can workers do when they're off work? In those days there was no internet, Wi-Fi or cell phones. The only connection with the outside world was a two-way radio contact in the office. So Luis acquired a 16 mm movie projector to show old black and white westerns, Laurel and Hardy, etc. Not too exciting, but that was their only entertainment.

Now I come onto the scene. Luis asked if I could come up to do a chalk talk and preach. Are you kidding? To this captive, rambunctious group of men? Would they jeer—or even listen?

Well, it was a chance to extend my mission outreach. Plus, I'd have a nice place to stay—and good food. So in the evening, I started to fly in as that night's featured entertainment. The only show in town! They were a captive audience, but they did actually seem interested in my chalk art and listened to my talks.

I decided, as an Added Attraction, to do a caricature of one of those guys. You know, draw his face, then add a cartoon body, depicting something about that person's character. The first night I asked a volunteer for this, they all whistled and called for this one guy to come up front and sit for my drawing. I knew that this guy had the reputation of being the toughest and meanest in the camp. *Why him, Lord?* Goodness knows how he might react.

Well, he came up front. His nickname was "Mono" which means monkey! What a temptation. Would I *possibly* dare to draw using the characters of that nickname? Would that burly guy physically attack me? Well, first I did his face. Then, very hesitatingly, I drew him hanging from a tree by his tail. He was posing beside me, so couldn't see what I was drawing. But the whole place was going crazy! Yelling, stomping their feet, bent over with laughter. Nervously, I took the picture off my easel and turned it around so Mono could see. I braced for his reaction. Slowly a big grin came on his face! He was actually proud of his new fame! He put that picture up over his bunk. Later Mono gave his heart to the Lord and everyone observed a tremendous change in him.

A GREAT GOLAZO

What on earth is a golazo? It's a sports term that I never heard growing up in Texas where football was king. I played from sixth grade all the way through high school. But after living sixty years in Latin America, I have been converted wholeheartedly to the 'other football', soccer. It is fast and exciting, a sport that people of all ages like to play. Alas, I apparently have two left feet which I could never get to cooperate in kicking a ball while running.

I confess that I did make *one* goal in all these years. But what a goal it was! Not to brag, but no one has *ever* come even close to that goal! It was what Latinos would call a 'GOLAZO!' (Spanish for a really stupendous goal.) So eat your hearts out, Messi, Ronaldo, Neymar, Pele, and Maradona.

Here's how it played out. Two of my friends in Guatemala were Norte Americanos, both successful businessmen and evangelical Christians. One was in the cotton business and ran a pig farm. The other had a cattle ranch. The cotton farmer had several airplanes used for aerial spray applications. He also had his own private single engine aircraft and a twin engine aircraft, an older model Aerocommander 690, but immaculately restored. He didn't fly, but would hire pilots to fly his planes. I flew for him on many occasions.

One day the other man called me, the one who owned the cattle ranch. He asked if I could do him a very special favor. "Yes. What is it?" He urgently needed to get a large sum of money to his ranch on the south coast. With the high crime rate in that area, driving down was out of the question. "Would I fly the money down?" He could borrow the twin engine plane from the other friend for the job. "Only one major problem," he added. "I don't have an airstrip on my ranch." I, of course, asked him what exactly he had in mind. First he reminded me that any halfway decent organization or business had a soccer field for their workers. So he had an excellent soccer field right next to the administration building.

He laid out his plan: I would fly the twin engine aircraft. It had a door right behind the pilot which could be removed. I would be accompanied by two workers from the ranch, one to show me the way, the other to shove a package with the money out the door the moment I shouted, "YAAH'. The money would be packed into a tight wad of duct tape, a little larger than a basketball.

Well, making a drop over a soccer field didn't sound like a big deal to me, so I agreed. We removed the door and away we flew. The man with the money-ball sat nervously near the door, tightly clutching this seat belt and the ball. We spotted the ranch and the soccer field with its official white strips and two goals. Seeing tall trees on three sides, I quickly formed a plan to get in as low and slow as possible, approaching from the treeless end of the field. I put two notches of flaps, dropped down to about sixty feet above the field at about eighty knots. As I came across, I made a wild guess and shouted at the top of my voice, "YAAH!" Out went the dough ball!

My only concern now was to avoid trees and stabilize the flight--no time to see where the 'drop' had landed. As I circled back around, down below was the administrator holding the ball and jumping up and down, as were a whole lot of other people. It seemed odd that all the villagers were running around, hands waving wildly in the air.

That afternoon, my friend called to thank me for the successful drop. What he added explained all the excited, waving villagers: "The package hit about mid-field, bounced once, bounced again and then went right into the goal! GOOOOLAZO!!!"

My stupendous soccer goal from an airplane!

GAS GENERATOR GOSPEL

When the government opened up free land to colonize the northern jungle, scores of people migrated north, forming new settlements. Since there were no roads, I helped several villages lay out locations for airstrips. In the process, I observed that many had no evangelical witness.

Devising a plan to evangelize these remote areas, I gathered the necessary equipment: a bed-sheet, a sleeping bag, my drawing board, a 16 mm projector, a few borrowed films and a small gas generator. After a day of my other flying duties, I often loaded that equipment and took off for one of those remote airstrips. As the settlers' workday ended and evening settled over the village, I positioned my noisy generator a distance away, set up the projector and hung the bed-sheet projection screen from the wing of the plane. That done, I prepared my drawing equipment.

When the sky darkened it was time to start showing a film. I didn't need to call them out. In a village with no electricity, the unaccustomed source of light brought them. Soon entire families filled the airstrip.

I began with short films from the embassy about hygiene or health issues. Next came a film about the life of Christ. Afterwards, using the light of the projector, I did my chalk talk, depicting stories from the Scriptures. I offered to pray with anyone. When the villagers disappeared back into the night, I crawled into my sleeping bag under the airplane and slept. (Later I had a pup tent.) Early next morning I packed up everything and flew back in time for breakfast with my family and another day of my usual flying. I did this as often as I could, visiting some villages many times.

That was decades ago. In 2017 the local Christian radio station interviewed me about my flying ministry. I told of this outreach. The next day I received a call from a young pastor. He was excited to hear my story on the radio because he had heard his grandparents tell how a pilot flew in to preach, draw pictures and share the Gospel.

The young pastor related that village now has a paved road and his church has over two hundred members. Then he invited me to come to speak at his church. Isn't it amazing how the Lord can work through some chalk and an ordinary gas generator?

BELLIGERENT BRAHMA BULLS

Woe is me! I had hoped my incident over cattle on the runway had fulfilled my 'incident quota.' Apparently not.

On this occasion, three pastors came to me and asked if I could take them out to a special church meeting. The church was in a beautiful valley, about a forty-five minute flight. The pastors had received permission for us to land on the airstrip of a large cattle ranch only a thirty minute walk from the church. Flying in, I spotted the airstrip. It appeared long enough for my plane, so I landed. Oh, that strip was an unexpected luxury. The owner of that ranch had his own airplane and kept his airstrip in immaculate condition. He had sown a special grass that he kept cut. It was like landing on a carpet.

The pastors said they would return in about three hours. Since I did not have a heavy flying schedule that day, I told them that I would wait there till they returned from their meeting, greatly reducing roundtrip expenses. I taxied to the far end of the strip.

With a book and some water, I was ready to enjoy a rest and the beautiful scenery. I propped myself up against a plane tire and started reading my book. As I turned a page, my eye caught sight of a little path into the jungle. Curious, I ambled over. To my pleasant surprise it led down to a beautiful cool, burbling mountain stream. No one was around, so I took off my shoes, rolled up my pants and waded out to about my knees. A refreshing experience in the heat of the jungle!

Upon my return to the airstrip, I discovered that we had company. At the far end of the strip five big Brahma bulls were munching and enjoying themselves. You know these bulls—tall, massive bulk, horns, big floppy ears and their distinctive feature, a huge hump on their backs.

As I watched from a distance, the munching bulls slowly moved closer to the middle of the airstrip. Knowing this would cause a serious problem for takeoff, I thought I'd mosey on down to see if I could shoo them off. As I walked closer, I discovered that they were not looking very happy with my presence. The first one eyed me, shook his head, grunted menacingly while pawing the grass. I got the message, backing off toward the airplane.

How on earth will I ever get those animals off the runway? At that moment one of the ranch hands appeared on horseback. Oh, salvation! I asked him if he would kindly remove those animals from the airstrip. He glanced in that direction and shook his head vigorously. He was not about to get involved with those animals, the meanest bulls on the ranch. He promptly rode off.

What now? At that moment the pastors appeared, eager to return to the city. After greeting them, I looked back. Oh, much, much worse! The bulls had lain down on the far end of the strip for a nice afternoon nap. Well, maybe if they stayed where they were, the plane could clear the obstacle. The pastors helped shove the plane as far back as possible—actually so far back that the tail wheel was in the bushes. Well, I would need every inch to take off over those animals. Besides needing lots of extra inches, this situation called for a "short field takeoff" technique-- one notch of flaps, rev the engine while holding the brakes, then let go at full power. *Okay, here goes!* The airplane strained at the brakes. I released the brakes, picking up as much speed as possible on the part of runway the bulls had left for me. When I felt I had enough flying speed I pulled up and off the runway.

Oh, no! The engine noise startled the bulls. They began to stand up! With a huge oomph, up first went their hind quarters, one by one. No time to gain more speed, this was it! I yanked the wheel back, barely lifting the front end of the plane higher into the air. As we passed over the bulls I heard a loud "whomp." What could that have been? We were still in the air and the engine was running fine, no vibrations. I looked out the window to check the wheels--no apparent damage.

Landing safely back in the city, a closer examination revealed nothing out of the ordinary. Puzzled about the source of the "whomp," I came to the conclusion that there was a Brahma bull back there with a tire mark on his hump.

QUICK CALF QUIZ

1. Can you carry in a small airplane a young calf safely?   Answer: NO
2. Can you carry in a small airplane a young calf? Answer: YES

QUIZ EXPLANATION:

To carry a young calf in a small plane is *never* totally safe. These procedures must be *strictly* adhered to:

FIRST: Take out two rows of seats.

SECOND: Cover the plane floor with a tarpaulin.
(We do not make potty stops.)

THIRD: Tie the legs of the calf together very tightly.
(Hint: Calf will not like this)

FOURTH: Lay calf down in the back.
(Calf is now getting uncontrollable.)

FIFTH: Seat a passenger next to you—with a pistol, loaded, ready to fire.

SIXTH: Give instructions to passenger: "If calf gets one leg free, use gun. BAM!" (It's either him or us)

Do *not* attempt to do this any other way!!

POPTUN PREDICAMENT

During the heavy guerilla warfare a call came for me to bring some missionaries in to safety from the jungle area where most of the military action was taking place. Looking out at the grey sky, I knew this wasn't going to be an easy mission. You see, in those days there was no weather satellite equipment, much less any kind of reliable weather reporting station. A pilot had only his compass and his watch to find his destination. And his eyes, if the weather was halfway decent. On this particular day, it wasn't.

To reach my stranded missionaries, I had to leave the blue skies of mile-high Guatemala City, climb above ten thousand feet and cross two mountain ranges before starting a descent down into the jungle area to the north. Usually the weather was gorgeous in the high country with small puffs of clouds clinging to the peaks of the mountains. After that, it was pure guesswork what the weather might be on the far side of the ridges.

My heart sank that day as I came across that last ridgeline and saw the entire jungle covered with a low layer of clouds. They looked fairly thick, with not much promise of finding an easy way through. But in my experience I knew the last hills before the jungle area usually offered some breaks to get down on the deck, so to speak. So I flew on. Sure enough, I spotted several small holes.

Down I went, exiting the cloudy overcast less than a thousand feet above the trees. Even down there, little ragged edges of clouds dipped into the tree tops. With a light mist falling, visibility was not good—at the most a mile—not much in a moving plane. At least there were no more mountains to contend with here.

I took what I thought would be the correct heading toward the landing strip at Poptun. Visibility worsened. I was seriously considering pouring on the power to climb out of this muck and head back to

Guatemala City. But those missionaries were counting on me. They had no other way out. I couldn't strand them out there with guerillas all around. So I pressed on a little further, desperately searching for the landing strip. At this altitude and visibility, I would almost have to fly directly over the white landing strip to see it. Even in good weather, a white strip was difficult to distinguish from the white limestone soil.

As I strained my eyes, I caught a glimpse of a patch of white on the right, standing out against the rich green jungle forest. Elated, I headed straight for that piece of white—it had to be the strip! Sure enough, it was the landing strip at Poptun. Fortunately, it was a long military strip and somewhat clear of potholes.

Unfortunately, I was flying in on a wide right base leg--not proper landing procedure. Desperate, I threw protocol to the wind. After all, who else would be so foolish to be flying out here on such a nasty day? So I buzzed right in, touched down and taxied to a stop near a small guard shack where my passengers would be waiting. I let out a sigh, thankful to get on the ground in such lousy weather.

Suddenly, as I was shutting down the engine, a huge military DC-3 dropped out of the sky and taxied in!! *Oh no! The pilot must have been on his final and I cut right in front of him! I never saw him.* How could I have missed a military plane large enough to transport Guatemalan Army troops? Well, it was painted in camouflage colors--who could have seen him against the jungle in this weather?

Still, I groaned, *I can't believe I just cut right in front of a military plane.* It is a very serious offence to cut *anybody* off on their final approach. All planes on final have the right-of-way! *Even worse, that is a military plane and we are in a guerilla war zone!*

I watched twenty or so fully combat-ready soldiers pile out of the huge plane, rush off to a truck and disappear in a roar. My heart pounded in my chest as I sheltered under the wing from the drizzle. I noted my passengers-to-be were detained by the military guards, but my mind was elsewhere. I braced myself. A moment passed and the pilot of the transport plane hopped out the door, dressed in a tailor-fitted flight suit, looked around and spied me standing there. Immediately he headed straight for me, taking off his flight gloves as he strode. He did not have a smile on his face, believe me!

As he came closer, I noticed the rank on his collar—a full colonel, no less! Now, friends, you need to know that in Guatemala a colonel is as high as you can go in the Air Force. And, no matter their rank, you *never* cross military people, especially in these dangerous times of internal warfare! This man could have me kicked out of the country, thrown in jail, grounded, plane confiscated and our flying ministry shut down forever.

"Are you the pilot of this plane?" he gruffly asked, looking me straight in the eyes. "Si, mi Colonel, a sus ordenes (at your service), mi Colonel," I humbly (and shakily) replied, slightly bowing as I said it. I stood there, trying to look as calm as I could, praying that the Lord would intervene in this tense moment.

The Colonel paused, just staring at me, it seemed for the longest time. I did not know what to say or do as he stood there staring at me. Finally, I noticed the countenance of his face begin to change as a perplexed look came on his face. Then he asked in a most polite way, "Say, are you that guy that draws on television?" Now it was me who had a perplexed expression. Could this hot-shot military pilot possibly have watched my program that we thought was only for kids?

He continued, "My wife never misses your program. She just loves the way you draw those pictures. She sure would like to know how she could get one of your pictures." Well, you better believe it, I offered right then and there to draw a picture and get it to his wife! We chatted a while before it fully hit me that I wasn't going to face military judgment. We parted and I got my passengers on board. Away we flew, up beyond the gray clouds to the bright blue, friendly skies of Guatemala City!

So I was able to keep flying but those early guerilla days transitioned into even more dangerous times. No one knew who was on whose side. Our mission work required flying into and over many areas that were considered real war zones. My activities appeared suspiciously like aiding and abetting the guerrillas--scouting out military movements, then reporting them to the insurgents. I was even accused by the government as being part of the communist takeover.

Their suspicions caused me to be constantly grounded, denied permission to fly. It played out this way: I would go to the offices of the Aeroclub to fill out my flight plans. The operator would inform me that I was grounded again. "Porque?" (Why?) No answer. I was to go to the Director and find out. This always required an unpleasant trip to make a personal appeal to the Director of Civil Aeronautics. I never knew if I would be detained there on some accusation or another. Just to go into that building stressed me immensely, my stomach tied in knots.

Now, once again, here I was coming to that building, hoping to get my name off this no-fly list. I walked in, headed for the stairs when I heard my name called. "Ey, Donaldson!" I turned and saw a military man in full uniform, braids and all. I didn't recognize him at first, but as he came closer, I realized it was the Colonel I had cut off on his final in the jungle at Poptun. I started to tense even more, but he greeted me warmly, asking "What brings you here today?" "I am here to see the Director." "Great," he said, "I *am* the new Director."

We climbed the stairs together to his office. I was ushered in to sit at his desk. Suddenly I remembered that I had not drawn that picture for his wife. Somehow it occurred to me to simply ask him what sort of picture she would like. I went home, drew the picture and next day took it to his office. I was ushered in and presented him with the drawing. He was so delighted, he called his wife. She wanted to talk to me, so we chatted a moment.

I left his office rejoicing how the Lord had been so gracious. The ministry had a friend, we still had a plane and permission to fly. On top of that, we now knew that, besides children, a great number of adults were watching our chalk-talk ministry program on TV.

MERCEDES MIRACLES

One time when my plane was being repaired, we scheduled a trip to the U.S. Our plan was to visit family in Texas and look for a reliable, affordable automobile. We would drive the newly-purchased car to California to visit the offices of MAF (Mission Aviation Fellowship). There we'd help expedite the process of combining MAF's flying mission program with ours in Guatemala. Then we'd drive the car home to Guatemala.

In Texas, a friend of my brother had a car that was available. It was an older model, a Mercedes Benz diesel sedan. The paint was faded, it had some scratches on it and a crack in the windshield. It did not look very good but it had low mileage, a very good engine, the tires were excellent and it was cheap. My brother's friend was practically giving it to me. Well, I knew I could get it painted in Guatemala at a very reasonable price. We bought the car.

We packed up the Mercedes, loaded in our little girls, about eight and seven years old, and headed out to California. Since there was no urgency, we planned to make this a real sightseeing trip, taking the back roads and enjoying the scenery.

On a small rural Texas highway Chiqui was driving. I was enjoying a brief nap when I sensed the car had stopped but the engine was running at the same speed. I immediately woke up and told Chiqui not to touch anything! She was just sitting there with a puzzled look on her face, her hands still on the steering wheel.

I moved to the driver's seat and tried to track down the problem. It appeared to be a transmission problem, one of those transmissions that had five forward speeds. At the moment it would not shift into *any* of those gears, nor into reverse.

So here we sat out in the middle of Texas on a small highway with no sign of civilization all the way to the horizon. Before long, a pickup drove up. The man offered to give us a tow twenty miles to Laredo, Texas, the nearest town. I was very hesitant. I knew that you should not tow an automatic transmission at a very high speed or the transmission could be damaged. Well, duh! That was the problem anyway, so it didn't matter. The man towed us to a transmission shop in Laredo where we signed the car in for repairs.

Now what? I called my brother and asked if he could possibly fly over and take us to his house. My brother operated a flying ministry from a little grass airstrip. Fortunately he had a four passenger plane. Back at his house, we sat pondering how we might get to California. We were scheduled to be there next week.

We didn't know. But God did. He helped connect us to a man in my brother's church who ran an aviation business. He had just purchased a new, very fast single engine airplane with retractable gear. He was incredibly generous to lend us his brand-new airplane to take to California. We were amazed, very grateful and accepted the offer.

So we arrived at MAF in California in a very nice four-place aircraft. I don't believe any missionary pilot had ever arrived at the MAF base flying such a fancy new airplane. It did raise a few eyebrows, for sure. But explaining our situation eased the tension and we had a wonderful time. We got everything accomplished that we intended before flying back to Texas to prepare for our trip home to Guatemala.

With no serious damage to the transmission, the car was repaired. It turned out to be a few rusted broken bolts that held the transmission to the engine. My brother flew me over to Laredo, I picked up the car, drove it back and we packed our stuff for our drive down to Guatemala.

Then I begin to have second thoughts about driving across the entire country of Mexico in a rather old car. If we did have problems, in all of Mexico at the time there were no Mercedes-Benz dealers, not one single agency or repair shop. I began to imagine what we would do if the car failed somewhere on those long, lonely roads in Mexico.

The more I thought about it, the more anxious I became. I wasn't sleeping well at night. If I were to have trouble somewhere out there, what would I do? I could not leave my wife and girls sitting in the car out in the middle of nowhere while I went searching for a mechanic. Neither could I ask Chiqui to get on a bus and ride into town alone to find help, with me staying with our two girls and all our belongings in the middle of nowhere. It was a real daunting dilemma.

By the time we set off to drive 100 miles to the border I was very distraught. As I crossed the bridge over into Mexico, my stomach was in knots, my stress level through the roof. I was praying fervently that the Lord would somehow get us through. We pulled into the Mexican Customs station and I went inside to begin filling out our papers to drive across Mexico. I noticed two elderly North Americans next to me having great difficulty in filling out these papers, since they didn't know any Spanish. I offered my help. They were greatly relieved and expressed great joy that I was there.

As we got their papers all in order, I casually asked them where they were going. They told me that their son was a missionary with the Mennonite church in Beliz (the country next to Guatemala). I asked if they had ever been there before. I could see the fear in their faces when they related that this was their very first time ever outside of the United States. They admitted that they were scared to death, with no idea what to expect.

Now here's the beginning of a miracle, though it is hard to believe. I asked them, "What are you driving?" They pointed to a pastel blue, brand-new Mercedes Benz sitting next to our car. I was incredulous. "That's the car that you're going to be driving?" They nodded. I inquired if they would like to follow me, since I was going to Guatemala. They could hardly believe their ears and immediately exclaimed, "Oh yes!"

So God provided an answer to their prayers and to our prayers! We drove out confidently, heading south with a brand new Mercedes-Benz right behind us all the way down to the turn-off where one road leads to Beliz and the other road to Guatemala. On that long trip, the only problem we encountered was a flat tire on their car. Another huge blessing was that they bought all my fuel as we traveled. I calculated that the entire trip from Texas to our home in Guatemala cost me a total of $5.50 for fuel. A bargain blessing!

Home in Guatemala I had the Mercedes painted and fixed up so it looked nearly new. It was cheap to operate and we drove it for a few years before selling it.

Thus, thanks be to the Lord who watches over us, we experienced several Mercedes miracles: I had a 'new' Mercedes car, a Mercedes companion through desolate territory, no Mercedes breakdowns and free gas for my Mercedes.

PETEN PITFALL

Pitfalls are lurking everywhere. Admit it. You have to dodge them every day. They are sneaky, appearing in a gazillion forms, many of them so subtle you don't recognize them till it's too late. The only positive thing about pitfalls is that one has an opportunity to mature through those experiences. As they say, "Live and learn." Aviation definitely emphasizes the *live*--IF you live, you can learn.

Latino life is a most beautiful life, with all its idiosyncrasies. Life is exciting, since you never know what is going to happen next. That is true everywhere, but amplified here. As a missionary friend of mine once remarked, "All permanent plans are temporary."

In Guatemala we have a word heard over and over every day, "Fijase." Technically that word comes from the verb fijar, to look at intently. It might be interpreted "If you look intently, you'll see it as it really is." For instance, you go to pick up your car after being in the shop for several days. The mechanic cleans his hands as he looks you in the face and begins "Fijase, your car is not ready. You see, my mechanic who does that, his mother-in-law was sick and you see........." I have learned over the years that if someone starts with the word 'fijar', it means you're not going to get what you came for! Count on it.

Some of that is excuse-making. But most is pushing the limits of lying. Doesn't it just seem second nature for a lie to 'just slip out'? Even among those who profess to be followers of the Lamb? Possibly even a missionary flying bush in Latin America?

Now it gets personal. A group of missionaries were opening a medical clinic and a church in the jungles to the north. They came to request a flight to that project. I had flown them several times to a strip at Sayaxche. Later I found out that the airstrip where I dropped them off was still a very rough four hour drive out to their clinic.

That day I was again flying them to Sayaxche. It was a clear day, so they asked if we could circle over the clinic to let them know they were on their way. I followed the instructions they gave me and soon spotted the little clinic cut out of the jungle. To my surprise I also saw a very straight path leading from a dirt road right to the clinic. The path had two sets of tire marks where cars had been driving. The trees on either side were cut back to where it seemed the wings of the Cessna would fit just nicely in between.

I asked my passengers about the surface condition of that little path. They assured me that it was without ruts or chuck holes, very firm white limestone soil. It seemed long enough and straight enough, so I asked if they would like to land at the door of their clinic. "Do you think we could? Oh that would be wonderful!" So I swooped down and made several passes over the path. It seemed in good shape. It hadn't rained in a day or two, so it should be firm.

Banking into the wind, I told them this was it-- we were going to land on that path. I put in full flaps, slowed the plane down. The approach was good. Actually, not as bad as some of our regular strips! I was lined up and the main wheels touched down to a smooth, firm surface. We came to a gentle stop right in front of the clinic, not more than fifty feet away from the front door! How was that for service? To your door! They were overjoyed. What a relief not to have to make that four hour drive over dusty, muddy, bumpy roads after an hour flight from the city.

Since the plane and I were there, they asked if I could take their power plant back to the Capital for some repairs. "Sure," I said, "no problem." With only me aboard there would be no weight problem. I tied down the power plant just behind my seat. I was ready to go, engine cranked up, check list done, all systems 'go' for takeoff.

'Short field technique' was called for in this situation, so I held the brakes and gave it full power, enough to lift the tail wheel slightly off the ground. The plane was straining against the brakes, waiting to surge forward and lift smoothly off to climb-out. As I released the brakes, the plane lunged forward, pushing me back into my seat, very normal for that power setting.

All of a sudden, the rail that held my seat in place gave way. My seat and I tumbled backward against the power plant, my feet up in the air. With the wheel still in my hands, the plane lifted off prematurely, trying to climb straight up. I was frantically struggling to reach the throttle but my seat belt held me down. Feet up in the air, no rudder control, the plane was headed into a stall. I felt totally helpless--I couldn't shut the engine down or control the aircraft. It was flying on its own!

At that steep angle, it didn't take long for the plane to stall about fifteen feet in the air. Then it veered off to the right and into the trees. Fortunately, there was no fire. I released my seat belt and climbed out. I hadn't even a scratch, but the plane sustained damage to both wings, with some damage to the cowling and upper fuselage.

Now what to do? I had no radio on the plane. And remember, the generator was with me, so the clinic had no electricity. The only way to get help was to somehow get in touch with my wife who could then contact authorities. I had only one option. I took that small path and walked to the little dirt road, about a half mile away. Soon a pickup came along and gave me a ride to the main road where I hitched another ride to the city of Flores.

Although Flores is where the main airport for the northern jungle was located, I could only hope to find a plane there. In those days what they called a regional airport was just a long dirt strip with a small shanty as a terminal building. Amazingly, as I arrived at the airport I saw a DC-3 warming up his engines. I ran toward the plane waving my arms above my head. The pilot saw and recognized me. He held his take-off.

The plane was one of those 'rubber airplanes' hauling rubber from the jungle to Guatemala City.

These are truly brave pilots, flying beat-up old DC-3s with no passenger seats, just full of big round loads of rubber gathered from the forests of northern Guatemala. These guys fly in all kinds of weather in their dilapidated aircraft, landing on strips rough-hewn out of the jungle.

Well, this pilot motioned for me to go around and climb aboard. Just as I managed to crawl over the big tubs of rubber, we were roaring down the runway on takeoff. I pulled myself into the cockpit and sat in the jump seat. After we settled in at altitude, the pilot asked me, "What were you doing running around out there without your plane?" I told him I'd just had an accident in the jungles. Now, we pilots are a close knit bunch and only another pilot can understand the turmoil of emotions surging through me. He asked me where. The accident site just happened to be right on our way to his destination in the Capital. He decided to fly over and have a look-see. He saw my plane in the trees, people standing around on the narrow path where I had taken off.

Understanding my humiliated feelings, he said, "Here, fly this thing back to Guate. Go on. Sit here and take the controls." I had always loved these old DC-3's, so I eagerly took the controls. We droned along with time to talk. He quickly got serious. "You know, it is against the law to land on roads or paths or anything that is not a legally registered airstrip here in Guatemala. They can take your license away, ground you for good or even kick you out of the country for reckless operation of an aircraft. You are in bad trouble Donaldson, bad trouble."

Now even getting to fly a DC-3 wasn't making me feel better. I was in a terrible situation. At that moment, his face lit up. " Aha! I know a way out of this. All you have to do is to tell the authorities that you were flying out there in the jungle and had engine trouble. You tried to make a forced landing on that little narrow path and you crashed! All the other pilots will think you're a hero, surviving a crash in the jungles. Best of all, you will be in good standing with the authorities. No one will know. You will come out of this smelling like a rose!"

Try to put yourself in my shoes. What would you have done? My flying career, my ministry, life as I knew it--all were hanging in the balance. My thoughts churned around in my head: *That is what I must do, to make this come out for the best for my family, my ministry, my service to the churches, my service to my Lord. I just have to tell a little lie, that's all.*

So much is in the balance. Oh, what shall I do? Tell that lie and save my neck? Or should I tell the truth and suffer the consequences of losing everything?

I will tell you what I did. Upon arriving in Guatemala City, I caught the inspector of civil aeronautics just closing up his office. Not only was the timing bad, but this guy had a sour disposition and a really bad attitude toward gringos.

Ignoring all that, I barged ahead and told him I needed to talk to him. I had just had an accident! He took me into to his office to make an official declaration about what happened. Details, please, where, when, how, etc. I put a sorrowful look on my face and sadly told him. "Señor, Inspector, I was flying out in the jungle. I experienced engine trouble and tried to make a forced landing on a road and I crashed into the trees. No one was hurt, for which we are thankful. Sir, that is it!"

Yes, I lied. Me, a missionary, a servant of the Lord Jesus Christ, someone people looked up to as a faithful witness of the God of Truth, yet I lied! He thanked me for being prompt in reporting the accident and promised to send out an inspector the next day to write up a report. As I left, he congratulated me on the fact that no one was hurt

My poor wife knew nothing of the accident until I got home and told her. I tried hard to smooth over the part about the lie, putting her at ease with the fact that I hadn't been injured, the plane was repairable and no one was hurt.

I didn't sleep that night, with the fires of hell burning all around me. I tossed and turned. Dear Chiqui supposed I was suffering from post traumatic shock, after wrecking an airplane in the jungle. But, no. I was suffering alright, but not from the accident. "You lied, Donaldson, you lied," kept coming before me all that night. Oh, I was so miserable. The unrest in my soul was terrible! I was under incredible conviction.

I arose very early, got dressed and called the inspector at his home about a quarter to six. "What are doing calling me this hour, can't it wait until nine o'clock in my office?" "No," I said emphatically, "I must see you immediately!" We both arrived at the deserted offices of Civil Aeronautics. He ushered me into his office and said, "Now what was so important that you had to get me out of bed and come down here at this hour? What is it with you Donaldson?"

I took a deep breath and confessed, telling him emphatically that I had lied and could not live with my conscience, or my Savior, for that lie. I had to tell the truth, let the chips fall where they may. "That is the true story, sir."

He just sat there with his head down, stunned at what he had just heard from my lips. I was thinking, *He doesn't like North Americans, so here is his chance to really let loose and vent all his hatred. He is going let me have it for sure. Get ready for a real chewing out and severe punishment for violating their laws.*

Finally after a long silence, he spoke ever so softly and said, "I have never heard anyone tell me the truth as you have. I don't understand it. You have done something I do not know how to handle." He picked up the report of the accident, and began to tear it into little pieces, saying ever so gently, "Case closed, adios."

Now I was the one who was stunned! What a miracle! Even more blessings followed as I managed to salvage the plane, repair it and return it to service for many more years, with continued permission to fly. More importantly, I could live with my conscience.

CANYON CATASTROPHE

This term of ministry actually began really well. Missionary Aviation Fellowship (MAF) wanted to extend their work to Guatemala. They elected to work under our umbrella, since our organization already had all the necessary governmental approval. MAF sent two pilots and two airplanes, along with their families. Our coalition led to good mission results and friendships. One pilot had children our girls' ages and our families had fun times together when I flew over to help out.

With three pilots and three airplanes, we had the entire country covered. I was based in the city, one pilot was based in Coban and one in Huehuetenango. Stationed in Huehuetenango was George Penner, a very good pilot who had been with MAF for quite some time. MAF was very strict about operating safely and George was designated as the safety officer for all of Central America.

Most of George's flying was to the north, crossing the highest continuous mountain range in Guatemala. He would fly from his Huehuetenango base at 6,000 feet, climb to about 13,000 feet to cross the mountain range, then down to 2,000 feet or less in the jungles. That meant a lot of flying miles and huge gas consumption.

One day George called me on the phone and said, "I've found a better route to the jungle, a short-cut through a canyon, so I don't have to climb up so high. I see only one drawback-- that area is controlled by guerrillas (communist insurgents) and they are shooting at me." I said, "Have they hit you?" "Yes I've got a couple of bullet holes in the airplane."

My plane, too, had had taken some shots on several occasions. We all knew a plane's aluminum body was not very thick, not much protection. Some time ago I had inquired as to how I could obtain a bullet-proof vest. That generated some anxiety in the mission. "What do you need a bullet-proof vest for?" If it hadn't been such a serious matter, my reply might have brought laughs. "I'm not going to wear it, I'm going to sit on it!"

The incident that had seized my attention was a bullet that missed the back of my seat by just a few inches. It had gone right through the bottom of my plane and out the top. I figured that if the bullet had been about six inches forward, it would have come right up through my seat. They did send me a bullet-proof vest and I did sit on it.

So I warned George, "You be really careful out there. You know we are flying in very dangerous conditions. We're caught in the middle of a war." The guerrillas were after us. The other side, the Guatemalan Air Force, had also targeted us, suspicious that we were flying reconnaissance for the guerrillas.

Not long afterwards George told me, "I just can't fly through this canyon anymore. It's shorter, but I don't feel safe." He wasn't. When you fly through those canyons, the trees and houses are right alongside

158

you. Kids come out of houses to wave at you—or maybe it's a guerilla aiming a gun at you.

The other option, up and over the mountains, is hard on the engine and burns lots of extra gas. So George was serious about finding a safer canyon he could zip through. It wasn't long till he sent a message, "I think I've found a good canyon and I can make it through alright."

About a week later when I was in Huehuetenango, he said, "Come on, go with me. I'll show you that canyon." We got in his 185, and flew out to the canyon. It looked good, with only one sharp turn to the left at a very narrow place, referred to as a 'dog-leg'. Making that turn while flying low inside a canyon with mountains straight up on both sides could be very dangerous in poor visibility. So my assessment was, "George, I don't think there's anything wrong with this canyon, except never do it unless you have excellent visibility." "Don't worry I am not going to fly in there without proper visibility." Well, I figured he knew what he was doing. After all, he was the safety officer and set a very high standard for all of us.

So we trusted his judgment and experience. He well knew the dreaded 'hazy season' which lasted from the middle of April to the last of May, when the rains started. This haze was a bad combination of people burning their fields and the seasonal stagnant air currents. The smoke cut visibility so badly that by the middle of May forward visibility was absolutely zero. You could look straight up and see some blue sky. If you looked straight down you might see a bit of ground, but ahead everything was just grey.

Worse, sometimes stratus clouds formed but you had no clue the clouds were there. They blended in perfectly with the haze. Flying along, all of a sudden you were in the middle of a really dense cloud. Then you couldn't see up *or* down, horizons or mountains-- you couldn't see anything--an indescribably harrowing experience.

I hated flying in the hazy season. One strip I needed to fly into during that season was located in a canyon. I would come across real high. Looking down, I could see the airstrip. But by the time I got down to turn in, I could not see the strip, so I had to come back up, find it again, then let myself back down in-between mountains, hoping I found the strip that time. Oh my friends, this kind of flying is just incredibly stressful. You can't image it unless you've been there. But people out in the jungle are counting on your flying services-- sometimes their very lives depend on you.

On one of those hazy days, George was loading his plane for a trip into the jungle with seven people on board. He had put an extra seat in his 185 so that, in addition to the passenger in front, he could carry three in the middle and two in the back. Since Guatemalans are small, that wouldn't overweigh his plane.

For this trip he seated a man up front next to him. Directly back of his pilot's seat, next to the window, he seated Paulo, a wonderful Christian young man. The local school teacher was in the middle of that row, with a young pregnant lady by the other window. In the back were two young men. After George made sure everyone was buckled in, he took off.

Paulo, the young man seated just behind George, had often flown with him. Paulo didn't know much about flying, but he was sharp and knew the dangers of the haze. He survived the accident and related to us exactly what had happened.

He said George started up that new canyon. The haze was very bad. Paulo was looking out his window, watching the trees go by on the side of the canyon, almost level with him. As they reached that critical forty-five degree turn, they flew into a stratus cloud. All of a sudden everything disappeared. He couldn't see those trees. He couldn't see anything.

In the split second it took Paulo to react, he turned his head to look out the front window over George's shoulder. That very instant he saw trees coming right at them through the haze. Then a loud bang, a tremendous jolt and complete silence. That silence really terrified Paulo—roaring engine to nothing. No screams, moans. Dead silence.

Here's what had happened: At the critical point where George had to make that sharp turn, he flew into the stratus cloud, completely losing sight of the canyon. There was no room for maneuvering or flying up out of the cloud. With only a second or two from one side of the canyon to the other, at 120 mph the plane hit the wall on the other side of that canyon. The plane crashed down through pine trees to the ground below. The only survivors were Paulo, sitting in back of George, the pregnant lady sitting on the other side and one of the young boys in the very back.

Why did only one of those two boys in the back live? The fifteen year old boy was on his first flight and didn't know how to buckle his seat belt. George had reached through to show him how to buckle it, but the boy was shaking so badly that George buckled his seat belt for him. The brash eighteen year old wanted to show off. When they got in the air, he told the other kid, "Hey, take your seat belt off, relax, be comfortable. Look." He took his seat belt off. The younger one knew he wouldn't be able to get it back on, so he just left it buckled. That saved his life.

When the plane hit the cliff wall, the guy who'd undone his seatbelt kept moving at 120 mph and became a missile, flying straight forward. He went through the row of seats in front of him, killing the young school teacher as his body hurled right through her, smashing into the back of George's seat, still going 120 mph. George was killed immediately. The other man in the front also died immediately.

Paulo slowly began to assess their very desperate situation. The pregnant lady was obviously in bad shape (the seat belt had damaged her stomach and baby). The young boy in the back was in total shock. Paulo struggled out of the wreckage, found that he had a bad cut on his leg but could walk. The plane had hit the ground at 11,000 feet in the mountains of Guatemala, wild country. Paulo began scrambling for help through brush up the side of the mountain. He didn't come across any roads but over a ridge he came to a small cabin. He told the people about the accident and pleaded for help. A man and his son hiked down to the plane. They pulled the pregnant lady out and carried her back up to their cabin, doing what they could for her. They headed back down to carry the young boy up to the cabin, leaving the four dead amid the wreckage. George was lying where he had been thrown out a little to the front of the plane, still strapped to his seat.

Nothing more could be done there. Paulo, with his leg badly cut, started walking out for help, even though they told him it was many miles to the highway. He began walking about four o'clock in the afternoon, struggled through the mountainous woods for three hours till he reached a highway about seven o'clock at night. He managed to hitch a ride the rest of the way to Huehuetenango.

Back at George's home base, no communication had been received from him. The young boy who worked for George in the hangar began to worry. He called me on the radio. "Hermano Don, George has not come back. It's now five o'clock. He was supposed to be back here by four and he's not back." I asked if he had called in. No, they had not received any radio communications. I tried calling George on the HF radio that MAF had installed in his plane. No answer.

I immediately went out to the hangar, jumped in my plane and took off, hoping to intercept an emergency signal. All our aircraft were now equipped with an emergency beacon. When something, even a sudden stop, activated the beacon automatically, it sent out a signal on an emergency frequency. I tuned to the emergency channel, then began to trace George's route, but above the haze level. It was like flying over an ocean, one great big mass of grey sea with only the mountain peaks visible. It was getting dark but I went all the way to Barillas, where I thought he might be, then circled back towards Huehuetenango. I didn't hear a sound, no emergency beacon anywhere. I turned and flew back into Guatemala City just as the sun went down. Any search and rescue effort would have to start the next day.

I called George's wife, Esther. She understood about the impossibility of continuing the search that night. She hoped, along with us, that perhaps George had encountered a problem but had safely landed at some remote airstrip, waiting for daylight. Maybe his battery had died, making it impossible to communicate.

But we decided to go ahead and notify George's MAF headquarters in California. The Vice President left on an overnight flight to Guatemala to take charge of search and rescue operations.

Visibility is always at its best early in the morning, so that's when rescue crews began to mobilize for what might be an extensive search. Aeronáutica took off with their helicopter and a medical crew. Our other pilot flew groups out to be supportive to George's family.

I left early for Huehuetenango to continue the search, following along the route that George and I had previously flown. When I got to that dog-leg turn, I spotted a wing in the trees at the bottom of the canyon. Immediately I called the Aeronautica helicopter to give them the exact location of the accident.

Then I flew on to Huehuetenango to wait for the rescue effort to report their findings. At about the same hour, a wounded and exhausted Paulo stumbled in the door at Huehuetenango, bringing us the bad news and details of the accident.

Not much later, the rescue helicopter arrived with three body bags, then had to return for the last victim. The Huehuetenango funeral home was summoned to prepare George for burial. I had the duty of inspecting each body bag to identify George. He was buried there in Huehuetenango. It was an incredibly painful time for Esther, the daughters and the entire missionary community. After winding up their affairs, Esther and children returned to California.

With the accident and increasing guerilla activity, it became much more difficult to continue our flying ministries. MAF now recommended that we reduce our flying presence to just one airplane which would operate out of our base in Guatemala City. So we closed down Huehuetenango and Coban bases.

AIR FORCE ATTACK

Guerilla warfare kept heating up dangerously. One never knew where or how they might attack next. But this day was just an ordinary flying day for me. I was to fly out from Guatemala City to pick up an Indian pastor and his wife who was having trouble with her pregnancy. The plan was for me to bring them into the city for medical care.

I had flown to this little remote jungle air strip before. It was next to a beautiful pristine lagoon in the middle of nowhere, no roads anywhere nearby. I landed on the air strip, right along the edge of the lagoon. Sure enough, there stood the pastor with his pregnant wife. I loaded them and their few belongings in the plane and we took off for Guatemala City. It was a beautiful day, white fluffy clouds, beautiful green jungle area below, mountains in the distance. I had no idea that just about 10 miles away the guerilla forces had ambushed a government military convoy. It was a major ground attack, with mortars, land mines, machine gun fire. The military convoy under this savage attack called for air support. Immediately the Air Force sent off a formation of their fighters.

While I was gaining altitude to Guatemala City, the Air Force planes were flying down to where I had come from. Our paths crossed! They were actually about 5,000 feet above me so I didn't see them, but they spotted me. Since my plane is painted white, I stood out quite clearly against that dark green jungle below me. I had no idea anything was going on--I was just flying along minding my own business.

Out of my field of vision, a couple of fighters had pealed off from the formation. Probably the instructions from their captain were: "Go get that guy, because he's the one that alerted the guerillas about our military convoys. He´s obviously been giving air support to the guerillas, passing along our movements. Go get him!" Still out of my sight, they dived straight at me. Suddenly my windshield was full of plane! I looked up and there was this jet plane about twenty feet in front of me, diving straight in! Though I hadn't heard anything, probably he´d been shooting at me. But when an airplane points his nose right at you, you know his intentions are not peaceful!

Whew! At the last minute he swerved, zooming down past me. Adrenalin was flowing, my knees were shaking in a terror of shock, scared absolutely to death. *What in the world is going on?* As I watched the jets fly away, I relaxed a bit. Oh, no! The two planes had turned and were starting back up towards me. *Those guys are after me! They're coming after me!* How could I escape before they started shooting?

I have always loved to read the exploits of air battles during WW II. Now I remembered an old tactic of pilots, ducking into cloud-cover to get away. Just ahead was a big white fluffy cloud. I headed straight into that cloud! But before I knew it, I was already out the other side. Frantically scanning the sky, I didn't see any planes. Yet to be safe, I flew right into the next set of towering cumulus clouds building up all around me. I breathed a thankful sigh, hoping I had lost those military jets. Apparently I had, so I continued on uneventfully to Guatemala City.

I called Approach Control, receiving routine instructions to land. I touched down. As I prepared to turn off the main runway, I called Ground Control for my usual permission to taxi to my hangar at the opposite end of the airport. I was stunned as the tower responded with, "Permission denied. Follow the military vehicle in front of you." I had seen the military jeep on the runway. That was nothing unusual. Since there was only one runway in Guatemala City, all commercial, military and general aviation aircraft used the same runway. But now this jeep sat on the runway, with several soldiers motioning me to follow.

Well, of course I had no choice but to obey and steer my plane over to the other side of the airport where the military base was located. They led me between two rows of hangars. Nervously, I noted it was a spot where nobody could see what was going on, completely hidden from view. As I shut down the engine, immediately my door was yanked open. Someone reached in, grabbed me and literally yanked me out of my airplane. Shoving me back against the plane, he pulled a pistol out of his shoulder harness, jamming it into my face and yelled, "SHUT UP!"

Shocked, I realized then what was going on. In those dark guerilla days, the government had "death squads" dressed in suits with shoulder holsters, driving new Jeep Cherokees. Their primary purpose was to track down any subversive sympathizers. This guy thought I was one. And I thought he was going to give me a couple of blows across the head with the barrel of his gun. He was very, very, mad. If you haven't been there, you have no idea what it's like to be up against real hatred--so thick you can almost cut it with a knife. Furious, these guys began to tongue-lash me.

Meanwhile men pulled out the Indian pastor and his pregnant wife on the other side of the plane. I could hear them giving the couple a rough time and going through their luggage. I never did know what happened to that poor pastor and his wife.

The soldiers started ransacking my plane, looking for any evidence that might incriminate me. I kept trying to say, "Call Colonel Cifuentes." (My uncle by marriage.) I was again threatened, "Shut up! Don't even open your mouth!"

At that moment, two of the men grabbed my arms, shoving me inside some sort of office. The room had nothing in it but a desk and two chairs. They ordered me to sit down, then left me there all alone. About an hour passed. Nothing. Nobody. I just sat there, uneasily wondering what was going to happen next. Finally a lieutenant from the Air Force walked in with a briefcase under his arm. Sitting down behind the desk, he began to ask me questions. "Your name?" Told him. "Address?" Told him. "Cedula I.D. number?" Told him.

Next, he dramatically pulled a folder out of his

briefcase and opened it on the desk. Questions came hard and fast. I was shocked. In that folder he had every bit of information about me and my family: where my daughters went to school, what grades they were in, what time they left the house, what time they came home, what my wife did. Another file detailed my work, where I flew to and what I did. Even more— notes about what they *thought* I did, suspected I did. He started reading it all aloud and interrogating me.

Then he asked for my cedula (identification card which all Guatemalans must carry on their person). I gave it to him and he put it in his briefcase. Now it's against the law in Guatemala for any policeman or soldier to take your cedula away from you. They can look at it, examine it, read it, copy information. But they cannot take it away from you. That is the law. They must hand it back to you. But this guy kept my cedula. Then he asked for my driver's license.

Fortunately, I didn't know then what I was later told by our secretary of operations, a young university student. He was fairly savvy about the operations of death squads. "That's their tactic," he said. "They grab you, take away your cedula, then tell you you're free to go. Relieved, you walk out on the street. Meanwhile, they radio some other guy who will stop you and ask to see your cedula. Of course you don't have it and of course it's an offence not to have your proper identification. They grab you, take you away and that's it. You are through, done-for, probably dead, because you have no proper identification."

I didn't know all that then. But this man *had* confiscated my cedula. After an hour or two of interrogation, he told me they would detain my plane but I could go. I had to walk home since my car was in my hangar, where I wasn't allowed to go now. Fortunately, we lived near the airport. I walked safely home. No death squad—this time.

The situation was getting very serious, for me and possibly my family. So, I decided to call my Uncle Fernando who had been promoted into the Ministry of Defense. Actually, he was now the second in command, right under the Minister of Defense, who was the most powerful man in Guatemala, The Man, the General, the head of the entire military force. Uncle Fernando was his assistant. I called him on the phone and told him my frightening situation. I was encouraged when he said, "Let me see what I can do." He did indeed intervene for me. To make the story short, he was able to get my plane back and permission to continue to fly. All my papers were returned to me, including my cedula.

However, life was definitely not "back to normal." From then on, we lived very cautiously. Every time we left the house we looked to see if we were being followed. Obviously not a pleasant way to live. Yet the situation continued to deteriorate even more, making it increasingly difficult to continue my flying ministry.

I was in an ever-tightening vise, being 'attacked' by both the government *and* the insurgents. The Guatemalan military put me on their 'watch list' as an agent for guerilla activities. The insurgents saw me as a spy for the CIA and declared they would soon catch me and have me killed. At that time, administrators from MAF, with which we coordinated our flying mission work in Guatemala, had suggested that we seriously consider the possibility of leaving the country.

Now we needed to do that. Our departure would leave the country with only the Guatemala City base. But that would be in the hands of a competent young Guatemalan pilot.

With MAF we formulated plans for me to be 'on loan' to fly for them for a term of five years. MAF administrators gave me a choice of several countries where they had openings in their aviation programs.

Chiqui and I decided on Ecuador and began the process of preparing for a major change in our lives. Though it saddened us to leave our Guatemala homeland, we breathed easier as we packed our bags to begin the move to Ecuador.

THE AMAZING AMAZON

I would now fly over other trees and canyons in another jungle. However, before we left Guatemala, a staffing problem developed at the MAF air base in Ecuador. Until solved, we were to go to Florida.

So we re directed to Miami to work at the MAF base at the Hialeah airport, flying to the Bahamas and Caribbean. They were operating with a Beechcraft twin engine aircraft and --to my great surprise-- of all things, the iconic airplane of all time--the famous 'Gooney Bird'! (Better known as a DC-3.)

What a thrill to be able to fly that great aircraft of World War II fame! I was checked out as a copilot and paired with a wonderful World War II pilot who had flown that legendary aircraft in the Pacific. He had recently retired from flying 747s to all points in the world. What a joy to co-pilot with someone who had so much knowledge and so much experience. However, I did have to learn and abide by his unique tactics for a very disciplined cockpit—specific hand signals for raising the gear, lowering flaps and many other operations.

During the six months that we lived and worked in Miami our family had one especially memorable experience. A pilot at the MAF base invited me to speak Sunday night at his church, a Presbyterian church in Coral Gables. I was a bit surprised, thinking, *That doesn't sound like a Presbyterian Church, holding Sunday night services. It must be just a small gathering of people.*

The pilot gave me the church address. Sunday evening we loaded up the family to go to the church where I was to speak. We found the street, but in the darkness we couldn't see numbers, so we just began looking for a church. First we came across a beautiful church with a very high steeple, all lit up with beautiful gardens. We admired it, but kept driving looking unsuccessfully for the small Presbyterian Church, where I needed to be—soon. It was getting late, almost seven o'clock. So we turned around to see if we had missed the church. Perhaps it sat further off the street than we were looking.

When we got back to the big church, we stopped to ask directions. Several men were waiting by the curb. One quickly opened my door, urging me to come with him immediately. Apparently, to my complete astonishment, this was the church where I was to speak! Another man slid into the driver's seat and took off with my family to park the car.

I was led hastily through the basement of the church, down long corridors, dark hallways and finally to a small stairwell. I was informed that big beautiful church, Coral Ridge Presbyterian Church, was pastored by the well-known Dr. D James Kennedy. I was to go up that stairs, open the door and just step out onto the platform. Dr. Kennedy would be sitting there waiting for me. He was. I barely recovered from my shock in time to present a message about the mission work in Guatemala.

After those six months in Florida we packed our stuff again and took off for Ecuador. Our flight landed in the capitol city of Quito, surrounded by beautiful mountains. A pilot from the MAF base in the jungle was waiting to fly us to our new home far out in the jungle. Thus our first views of Ecuador were quite dramatic, flying from nearly two mile high Quito, through a narrow valley, turning amid the volcanoes, down to the tiny jungle town of Shell Mera at 3,501 feet altitude. After landing on the well-kept asphalt runway, we were driven past the few tumble-down shops to the other side of the road where the old tropical hospital and wide-eaved wooden houses stood.

Isn't it just like the Lord to transform painful things into great things? Yes, we were sad about having to flee our country, family and ministry, ending up in this far away "nowhere" place in the jungles of the Amazon. But God filled the next four years with so many blessings that we look back upon that time as being one of the great blessings we have had in our ministry.

We met many wonderful people. One was Rachel Saint, the sister of jungle pilot Nate Saint who was speared to death with four other missionaries in 1956. We also became acquainted with some of the wives of those other martyred missionaries.

The tragic story had been amazingly followed by the courageous return of Betty Elliot, wife of martyred missionary, Jim Elliot, and their young daughter, along with Rachel Saint, to live with the Auca/Huarani tribe who had killed their loved ones. Their mission was to show the Huarani the way of forgiveness and saving faith. This saved not only souls, but the Huarani tribe which had nearly been eradicated by revenge killings.

A truly great blessing was to actually meet and get to know three of the Huarani men who had killed the missionaries. The three 'killers' are now preaching and reaching out to their own people still living in the far reaches of the jungle.

I had the privilege of flying those three Huarani men out to many remote jungle locations, leaving them at some old airstrips which had been abandoned after the oil companies departed. I would return in a week to pick them up. Since they did not speak Spanish, Rachel Saint would translate, telling them when I would pick them up. On my return, they were always at the landing strip, right on time. The flights saved them days of treking through jungle, so they expressed their gratitude by sometimes presenting me with a live monkey--a real sacrifice for them, since monkey was their favorite meat. It wasn't on our menu.

Way out in that eastern jungle in Shell Mera was one of the finest hospitals that you would ever find anywhere. A project of the radio ministry HCJB, it had been the vision of the martyred missionary pilot, Nate Saint. In addition to his flying ministry, Nate started a church and a school, then noted that there was no medical care for people in the entire eastern jungle. He and Dr M. Everett Fuller raised the funds, bought the land, built a single room clinic, then 'birthed' a full care hospital. Surgeon Dr Fuller, with his wife Liz who was a nurse, administered the hospital as long as his health allowed. The hospital was primarily staffed by missionaries from many parts of the world, along with Ecuadorian nurses and occasional Ecuadorian doctor.

Flying sick and wounded people from the jungle to the Shell hospital constituted a great deal of an MAF pilot's work. Without the planes, people might walk or pole a dugout canoe for two or three days to get a sick or wounded person to the hospital. We also flew the recovered patients (and any deceased) back to their villages.

Early on, I was cautioned about a jungle custom. When we would land at a remote airstrip, the villagers, to show their gratitude for our service, would often greet the pilot with a small pottery cup of the jungle drink called 'Chicha'. I was strongly advised not to drink the stuff, yet I didn't want to insult the people's hospitality. So I would put the cup to my lips without taking a sip, smile and thank them.

The reason for this severe warning: Chicha is made from yucca (cassava or edible white sweet potato). After peeling and dicing, the yucca went into a really huge pot over an open fire. The ladies of the village then sat around the pot, chewing pieces of yucca, spitting the masticated yucca back into the pot— of course, mixed with their saliva. The heat and saliva quickly caused fermentation. After seven days the brew was pronounced ready to drink. Hmm. Wonder if that might have any connection to the high rate of tuberculosis in those villages? Tubercular patients, along with snakebite victims, were the two most common medical conditions we flew to the hospital.

Flying over the jungle, it didn't take me long to notice one dramatic contrast with Guatemala--no one was shooting at me. However, I don't remember a single Ecuadorian day when I was not flying in rain. At the MAF base the average rainfall a year was twenty-two feet. If it wasn't raining at the base, it would be raining at the destination or somewhere enroute. If you don't like flying in heavy rain, don't fly in the Amazon jungle.

However, on a clear day, looking down on that vast expanse of Amazon jungle was always an incredible experience. As far as you could see there were no roads, no houses, no open fields, not one sign of civilization. It looked like an enormous garden of broccoli plants.

Navigating over those broccoli tops in the days before GPS or other navigational aids, we flew IFR, humorously translated means 'I follow rivers'. Actually, the aviation term IFR signifies 'Instrument Flight Rules'. You're guided only by your instruments and, if you're fortunate, a river. VFR, the opposite term, signifies 'Visible Flight Rules'. You can see villages, buildings, runways, mountains and cleared land down below to aid you in navigating by sight. Most days, though, we had to fly "I Follow Rivers" over those endless broccoli tops. That meant we took off, picked up a river, followed it until we had to turn to cross over to another river (or more) to follow till we spotted our destination runway.

I will never forget my first flight out of the base in Shell. We received a call from some missionaries at a station far out in the jungle. I had never been there but I was told that it would be easy to find. It was on the main river, had a radio station with a high antenna and some buildings.

That sounded pretty easy, so I took off on the heading that they gave me. I picked up the river but soon found a complete fog-cover over the rest of the route, as far as I could see. I flew up over the fog, not able to see the river, but kept on that direction until I picked up a signal from the radio station. With that, I navigated to the destination. But upon arriving I discovered that only the top of that radio antenna was sticking out of the clouds, no landing strip in sight. I circled around a bit hoping for an opening in the clouds. I finally had to turn back toward our MAF base. Getting back was no problem. I could navigate by several familiar snow capped volcanoes rising above the fog. I headed for the middle peak which gave me a heading for the airstrip.

Now a short diversion to emphasize why "I Fly Rivers" is so absolutely vital in the jungle. The jungle has three layers: the top layer is made up of leafy small branches, the second layer has bigger, leafier branches, the third layer is dense jungle ferns, vines, brambles. If you were to go down due to a mechanical problem, your plane would disappear in the top layer and never leave any kind of mark on the jungle. If someone flew over looking for you, they would have no clue to where you had gone down.

If you survived the crash, you would be in your plane about 30 or 50 feet above the ground. Climbing down would be quite difficult, especially if you had broken bones. Even if you did get to the ground, you wouldn't have much of a chance of survival in that hostile environment of poisonous snakes, scorpions, tarantulas, jungle preditors and brambles.

Our family time in the Amazon wasn't all about flying. We enjoyed church, family get-togethers, games of soccer on a dirt lot, as well as special celebrations.

We were incredibly fortunate to be in Ecuador when local churches were planning a memorial of the 30th anniversary of the martyred deaths of the five missionaries by the Huarani Indians.

The council of Evangelical churches had organized an outdoor presentation in a public park in the large coastal city of Guayaquil. The missionary radio station HCJB would transmit the service worldwide. The program included musical groups and singing. Along with the director of a local seminary, I was asked to bring the message. But the main attraction was the presence of three Huarani men, with Rachel Saint to interpret for them. The 'podium' for the service was the platform of a flatbed truck.

Quite a crowd gathered. The people of Guayaquil were fascinated by these 'savages' from the jungle. At the end of the service the announcement was made that if anyone would like to shake the hands of these three men, they could come forward. Hundreds pressed forward with their children on their shoulders, to hope to shake the hands of these 'savage killers' from the dense jungles of the Amazon who, for decades, were known to the entire world as Aucas, a Quechua word meaning 'savage animals'. But the tribe calls themselves *The People*. That is, *Huarani,* in their language. When they give their testimonies, they always began by saying, "You see me here as a man."

It was amazing to observe the tremendous interest and curiosity the Ecuadorian people had about the jungle and its inhabitants. Few had ever ventured into 'those dangerous jungles' so knew only horror tales about primitive savages. The opportunity to shake the hand of one of these men was a memorable life experience for them.

Other non-flying events awaited me. A classmate of mine from college days was a missionary in Ecuador. He invited me to preach in several different churches. As we ventured to these locations, I saw many different parts of Ecuador. Once he took me to a very remote location high in the mountains. We were thankful to be in his pickup truck as we drove through very heavy snow. Yes, even though Ecuador is on the Equator, there is still some very icy weather high up in the mountains.

Another time I was called to be the speaker at services in the mountains. It was extremely cold and services were held in a tent. In spite of discomfort, there was a moving of the Spirit. The pastor informed me that that several people wanted to be baptized, so we trooped to a small lake on the outskirts of the village. You can imagine, I was *most* thankful to find that the visiting district director of the mission was asked to do the baptism. We gathered on the banks of that small lake on that cloudy, cold day. The water was shallow, so they had to wade about 100 yards through icy water to get to water deep enough for baptism. It did not seem to bother them. Elderly men and women and young people were baptized. It was a joyful service and a wonderful blessing.

Near the end of our time in Ecuador a need arose at the Alliance Academy in Quito. The head of the art department had to make an emergency departure. The administrator heard of my artwork, so he asked if I would come up to be the art teacher for the Academy that year. Chiqui was asked to be a Spanish teacher and I would also take one of the Bible classes for the middle school. Arrangements were made for MAF to release me from flying. It meant that we would have to move again, but it was a wonderful time for us. Our two girls were able to attend this wonderful Christian school with students from missionary families throughout South America.

Living in Quito also allowed us to become well-acquainted with one of the great missionary outreaches of the world, the radio ministry of HCJB (Heralding Christ Jesus' Blessings). On the outskirts of Quito, nearly two miles high in the mountains, HCJB had engineered what they called the 'Antenna Farm'. A maze of huge antennas of all shapes sent shortwave signals to the entire world. Missionaries located in various parts of the world prepared Gospel programming in many different languages to broadcast to far distant lands. HCJB also operated a local TV station with studios in Quito. I was invited several times to do chalk talks and illustrations on programs.

So our years in the Amazing Amazon *were* amazing, even the dangers of flying low over rivers to navigate. Flying low reminds me of a story I heard about a man saying he would never fly in an airplane because it would be "against the Bible." I thought I knew the Bible quite well, but I wasn't aware of any prohibitions about flying. Where did he get that idea? His answer was that the Bible says, "Lo, I am with thee." So he felt God wouldn't be with him unless he stayed low on the ground. I chuckled when I heard the story. 'Lo' isn't exactly how I spell that word when flying.

Now, with our term flying in Ecuador with MAF completed, we moved back to Guatemala. We unpacked our belongings into our apartment in Guatemala City, which we'd rented out while we were away. Life in our beloved country was settling down and we were thankful to once again be near our wonderful family, friends and church.

Since the dreadful guerilla warfare was subdued, I was again flying over Guatemalan rivers. Instead of war zones, guns, holes in the plane, being on two 'watch lists' and no-fly orders, the main dangers in flying came from nature: clouds, storms, mountains, the dusty season and narrow canyons.

TIRELESS TRACTOR

No, this isn't about a tractor without tires. It's more like an adult version of the old children's story *The Little Engine that Could.*

I was sitting at the Aeroclub eating a snack when a very agitated man approached me saying, "Do you speak English? They told me you speak English. Can I talk to you?" "Yes I do speak English. What is the trouble?" He related how he had recently come to Guatemala to help in the earthquake relief effort. He was given a large sum of money for a project he would designate. But an emergency had arisen and he had to return to the USA immediately. There had been no time to find a project. He asked me if I had one that could use the money.

For some time I had been contemplating a plan for one area where I had been flying. I described that project. Desperate to complete his trip successfully, he signed over the cashier check to our AGAPE mission, a sum of $8,000.00. In those days that was a great deal of money. He thanked me profusely before he hurriedly left to catch his plane.

Here is what was in my heart at that time. I had opened three airstrips in a remote mountain valley in north-western Guatemala for the two churches ministering there, the Primitive Methodist and the Mennonites. This valley had only one road which was passable only in the dry season. There were no buses, no trucks or cars. Over the years I had observed how the farmers in that area prepared their fields for planting. They were using oxens pulling a single-tree plow. After six months of no rain, the ground would become very hard and thus extremely difficult to plow.

I am not a farmer but was always interested in farming. I began to imagine how a small tractor could be a great help. Now that I had some funds available I decided to look into the possibility of acquiring a small tractor for shared plowing in this valley.

I made a trip to the Kubota dealer in the city to seek information. To my surprise, they had a great line of tractors, from very large to small ones. The agent told me what would probably be the best-suited tractor for what I was describing to him. It was just a little larger than a riding mower in the States. It came with a blade in the front and a three-point hydraulic connection in the back which would serve to be able to hook up several different implements.

On my next visit to the San Andres Valley I asked for a meeting with some of the leaders of the two churches to present my plan to them. After forming a committee to oversee this project, they would begin by designating a young man to learn to operate the tractor.

The tractor and driver would be made available to any farmer for a small fee, the same that was charged to rent oxen for plowing. That money would go to buy diesel fuel, pay the driver a small salary and purchase any necessary parts. They all agreed on this plan. I purchased the tractor and made arrangements for the dealer to take it to the San Andreas Valley in their truck.

Finally the day came for delivery of the tractor. It was the dry season, so the trip was made with little difficulty. I flew the dealer's representative out to oversee the introduction of this tractor to the people. A small crowd gathered on this eventful day when mechanization would finally come to this remote valley.

The chairman of the project was the pastor of the Primitive Methodist church and the local pharmacist. Twenty year old Pasquale had proved he could quickly learn how to drive this tractor. For the next few weeks I flew out a man from the dealer to continue to instruct Pasquale on how to drive and operate this machine, along with how to plow a field. He had no trouble with that part as that's what he had been doing all his life, plowing fields.

That tractor provided a great service for all the farmers in that area and was a great testimony to the witness of Christ. For the next several years it was kept very busy and the project was very successful. When Civil War came into that valley, it was feared that the communist insurgence would find the tractor and burn it, destroying the whole project. So it was put in hiding in a remote house. I lost track of the tractor, since I couldn't fly into that war zone. Then we moved to safer flying with MAF in Ecuador.

After we returned from those years in Ecuador, we discovered a wonderful blessing. When peace had

returned to the area, the US government had sent two Peace Corps workers into the San Andres valley to help the farmers learn more efficient farming methods, teaching many of the farmers how to terrace their fields. The tractor proved to be a real boon for this work, using the blade on the front.

After several more years the next stop for this little tractor was the Bible Institute of the Primitive Methodist church located about 100 miles to the west in another town and another valley. There that little tractor labored in the fields of the Bible Institute. After many years had passed I totally lost track of that tireless little orange Kubota tractor. Could it still be chugging along somewhere?

MARVELOUS MKs

Now to fill in some of the blanks in our story. Chiqui and I were blessed with two beautiful daughters. They began life in Guatemala, living next door to their cousins, grandparents and other family members. They also began life already 'anointed' with several titles. The first MK title was as My Kids (Our Kids, of course). They were then automatically blessed with a second MK, Missionary Kid. But they were also PKs, Preachers' Kids. (Since I was a PK, does that make them PK Juniors?) Fourthly, they were also TOs, Theological Offsprings. So humorously, the oldest could have been referred to as Miss Donaldson, MK, PK, TO, PhD (a degree she earned as an adult.)

Seriously, growing up as a MK could be a very unique, and often difficult, environment. Many MKs endure years of stress of trying to sort out their identities. Are they the nationality of their parents' homelands or of the country where they grew up while their parents ministered? Worldwide MK conferences try assist in sorting through this quandary along with other MKs and counselors. Most of these young men and women live very 'normal' and productive lives.

Our own MKs have no identity problems. If you ask them, they are quick to answer, "We are Guatemalans!" They are! Half Guatemalan genetically, then Guatemalan by birthplace, rearing and schooling. They are very proud of their heritage and up-bringing.

At times that caused puzzled looks. They do not look Hispanic. Their last name is Donaldson. They now speak English flawlessly. Of course, they speak fluent Spanish without an accent. Inside they are definitely Latinas. They do not think or react like girls from the U.S.A.

The girls attended kindergarten and primary school in Spanish. Their mother talked to them in Spanish. As their father, I only spoke to them in English, but it was the only English they heard. Occasionally they did speak a little English (with a very heavy Spanish accent) to their grandparents living in the USA. When they were teenagers, after hearing me preach, they would correct my Spanish. They also tried to correct their mother's English. Now they have lived many years in America, but whenever they speak with their mother, they automatically switch hard drives and go into Spanish.

Because I spoke English to them, when they went to high school they made the transition into English with minimal problems. In fact, our oldest daughter earned a Masters in English and completed her doctoral degree in the USA, after graduating from a local Guatemalan university. Amidst all of this both girls graduated from Hebron Bible Institute in Guatemala City.

If you would ask the girls about their childhood, they would tell you how they loved to fly with their Daddy to visit the Indian villages. In one village where I was preaching, we stayed at a typical home--no doors, just a plastic sheet. We constantly had visitors all night, dogs, cats, chickens, piglets. Our four year old daughter described it perfectly, "Mommy, Mommy, this is like sleeping at the zoo!"

Often, however, I was leaving them behind. They needed to be in school; the plane couldn't handle extra cargo weight; I was flying in dangerous situations or into difficult village issues. So, on my final approach back into Guatemala City, I purposely edged over to fly above our house. I'd rev-up the engine, so they'd hear me coming in. If they were outside playing, they would call out, "Mommy, Daddy's home!"

Unfortunately, sometimes I did not make it home due to weather or mishaps. Then there came a time when I often didn't make it home for different reasons. I had become so busy that I was neglecting my family, missing meals, birthdays, other activities. I began thinking I was indispensable and needed to give all my attention to the ministry. It was a terrible mistake, but I was eventually brought up short by my five year old daughter. She was sitting on the steps that led up to our apartment when a group of Indian believers came looking for me, to request a flight. They asked my daughter, "Little girl, is your father home?" She turned around and shouted up to her mother, "Mommy, does Daddy still live here?" When Chiqui told me that, my heart was broken.

Not long after that, our family doctor called me in to his clinic. He was a very wise and sincere believer. He sat me down and gave me a good old fashion 'tongue lashing.' "Stop trying to be God's answer to the mission field here in Guatemala. Stop neglecting your family, they need you more than anyone else." Folks, I got the message!

When they were ten and nine we moved to the Amazon jungles of Ecuador, as recounted in the Amazing Amazon chapter. Many ex-patriots staffed MAF and the HCJB hospital. A school for the families consisted of a one-room school building and one teacher with about ten students from first grade to high school. On the first day of school, one of our daughters came home and happily announced, "Mommy, we are the most popular kids in school!" Apparently they adapted as quickly to life in the jungle as in everything.

In Ecuador I had often flown the three Huarani Indians who had participated in the killing of the five missionaries. Occasionally, they presented me a live monkey (their favorite food) as thanks for my airplane service. We never ate them, but found that these very small, docile monkeys made excellent pets for our daughters. One day when I came home, my youngest daughter had her pet monkey dressed in her doll's clothes, sitting in her doll stroller with its tail hanging over the end. It was gripping the little stroller with all his might and chattering as she pushed it. Quite a sight to behold!

During that time in Ecuador, an often-fatal epidemic of 'the jungle measles' broke out. That kept us very busy flying many villagers to the hospital in Shell Mera. Our daughters had received all of their immunizations, but evidently it did not cover this strain of measles. Sissel came very close to dying. It was incredibly difficult while she hovered at death's door for about a week. The entire missionary community and the local church were fervently praying for her. She survived with a total recovery! We surmised that I must have brought home the germs from all the patients I had been flying in and out of the jungle.

In Ecuador Chiqui was very desirous for the girls to continue their musical education. Chiqui had taught them piano. Now Almarie was learning the flute, while Sissel was playing the violin. There weren't music teachers in Shell Mera. Connected to the HCJB radio studios in Quito lived the finest musicians you would find anywhere. However, Quito was six hours away by bus on one of the most dangerous roads in all of Ecuador—a narrow dirt road with a solid rock wall on one side and on the other, an 800 foot drop-off, straight down with no guard rails. Meeting oncoming traffic, one vehicle had to back down a considerable distance to a wider passing area.

Chiqui made this frightening trip once a month with the girls. I never rested until they walked in the door! On one trip coming back at night, the small bus lost its headlights. So the helper hung out the door with a flashlight in his hand, supposedly providing enough light. They got home safely. And with these lessons, the girls became excellent musicians. I had my own orchestra to play as I drew my chalk art before preaching. Chiqui accompanied them on the piano. That beautiful chalk art music ended with the music of the girls' wedding bells.

The girls finished high school, one by correspondence from the University of Nebraska, the youngest from our church school in Guatemala. Then came the wider world, to which they easily adapted. Both of our daughters went to Botswana, Africa, for two years to teach at a mission school in Gaborone.

The girls' teaching jobs at the mission school were very unique. Many professional people contracted to work in Botswana from many different countries. To educate their children in English was a real plus. This multicultural mission school offered high-quality education from kindergarten to high school, with an emphasis on Christianity. The opportunities were incredible. In one class of first graders several children had never even heard of Jesus! Besides the joy of visiting our daughters, we also shared the Gospel in the school and the local Pastor arranged for me to speak in several churches and tent meetings in villages.

Several years later we visited Almarie in Hong Kong. She was teaching at the University of China in Hong Kong for one semester. She was accompanied by her two daughters who had been adopted from mainland China. In one class our daughter taught a group of young Christian ladies who had escaped from persecution in Communist China.

Chiqui and I went for one month to help out. Their living quarters across the street from the University were excellent. The train system was very efficient, so we took the girls to their Christian primary school by train, then picked them up in the afternoon. We chuckled at people staring at us, wondering why those two 'round eye' people were traveling with two obviously Chinese girls.

Almarie taught in English, since everyone wanted to learn English. I was fascinated with the students all using iphones, yet the phones didn't use the Chinese characters. They had developed a language called, "ping-ying," basically writing the sound of their words using our alphabet.

Today, both girls live in Virginia. One has seven children, the other has two adopted girls from China. They both are serving the Lord in different capacities. We are very thankful to the Lord for their lives and their commitment to the Lord.

NOT A WHITE MAN

A surprising 'Ah ha! moment' occurred during our visit with our daughters when they were teaching in Botswana.

While there, the local pastor arranged for me to speak in some churches and tent meetings. I would need an interpreter. He introduced me to Robi who could travel with me on the longer trips to tent meeting sites. Robi was told only that I was a pastor from Guatemala. He had no clue where Guatemala was. The only two places in the entire Western Hemisphere he'd ever heard of were the USA and Canada. I could have been from Mars, for all he knew.

With many hours together driving to villages, we had abundant time to talk. I began to sense that he, a black man, didn't consider me to be a white man. I was just someone from another third-world country. That allowed him to talk freely about some unpleasant experiences with white men.

I politely listened to his tales, never even hinting at my ethnicity. For those brief hours I was transformed into a person of another race. Missionaries over the centuries have desired such a connection, to be fully embraced by the culture where they were ministering. Now that amazing experience was mine.

At our tent meetings, I was introduced as Guatemalan. Without electricity, the services were *charged* by God's spirit with energetic singing, His power, plus enough daylight to see my chalk talks.

After one service an elderly man came up to me. Through Robi, he said that the Gospel was now clear to him. He first saw it in chalk drawings by someone who was not a white man, then heard it translated through Robi, a trusted Botswanian.

FINAL FLIGHTS

This chapter covers a lot of territory, roaming back through previous years. As I write, I'm still a missionary now, but not a pilot. These assorted flying adventures and tragedies all led to decisions we made about the final flights of my missionary years.

FLASHBACK: Headed for mission work in Ecuador, we had finished packing. Before we left Guatemala I heard that a very famous speaker was coming to speak. He would hold a service in a downtown Guatemala City hotel. Eager for this opportunity to hear him, I bought a ticket for the banquet. At my table were several Guatemalan business men. The man sitting next to me was the owner of the major flour mills of Guatemala. In our conversation, I discovered that, though not a pilot himself, he owned two airplanes. The planes were essential for his country-wide business. He had hired a professional pilot. I commented that I was a missionary pilot and handed him my card. We agreed the speaker was excellent and parted ways. Our family soon departed Guatemala for our contract with MAF (Mission Aviation Fellowship) in Ecuador.

FAST-FORWARD: Six years later, my term of flying for MAF in Ecuador was coming to an end. As yet, we had no definite plans for 'what next.' MAF offered us a position at their home office in California in the area of public relations, utilizing my experience preaching. A good offer, but we really did not want to live in the USA. It looked like we were headed back to Guatemala, but to do what?

Finding a ministry in Guatemala hadn't looked like a very viable option at that point. I had founded AGAPE (Association Guatemalteca Aeria Para Edificacion) in 1970 and managed it until we left for Ecuador. While we were away, the political situation had changed. AGAPE, as a nonprofit aiding in community development, should have been welcomed. But increasing government prejudice against evangelical organizations had made things quite touchy. Though still in operation, there was not any opening for me.

I certainly did not readily entertain the thought of continuing bush flying. I felt like I was getting too old for that sort of flying. Landing on those short airstrips (900 ft. of grass, mud, pot holes, animals), would be like driving your car into your crowded garage at sixty mph! Though I welcomed an opportunity to continue flying in ministry, in my mind was a vision of a more 'sophisticated' plane landing on two miles of smooth asphalt. So far nothing had opened up, certainly nothing as appealing as that 'dream job' in a state-of-the-art plane.

So we arrived back in Guatemala, jobless. Trusting the Lord for guidance, we began unpacking and moving back into our apartment, which had been rented to another missionary family. We hadn't been home a week when the phone rang. The voice and name were of a person whom I did not recall ever meeting. He refreshed my memory. Oh my goodness, Juan Carlos! (See Flashback) The card I had given him at that dinner meeting had lain for six years at the bottom of a drawer in his office. Exactly when he needed to find a Christian pilot for a ministry, he came across my card--definitely a 'God moment.' As a dedicated servant of the Lord, he wanted to plan and facilitate conferences for pastors all over Latin America using his aircraft. He needed a Christian pilot to fly missions in a Beechcraft Barron 58, beautifully equipped with twin engine, radar, etc.

Juan Carlos went on to explain that, in addition to the ministry part of the job, once in a while I would have to make business flights to the south coast where he had some farms. Also I would fly the administrator down to the port of Barrios to supervise the unloading of hard wheat from Canada. (Hard wheat, necessary for making bread, does not grow in Guatemala, so must be imported.)

It sounded like the perfect job—great plane, good runways and an interesting variety of operations. The Lord surely does work in wondrous ways. I signed on as the Christian to pilot his Beechcraft Barron. As the ministry grew, he upgraded to a fine pressurized twin engine Beechcraft Duke, making it possible to fly higher and maneuver around bad weather. As the ministry continued to grow, we were using both planes in his ministry.

We decided to attend the church where Juan Carlos and his family went. I was invited to speak occasionally. The church was a blessing for our family. Juan Carlos had two daughters the same age as our daughters, so we had good family fellowship. Another good connection was the church's missionary, a fellow pilot with a Beechcraft Barron.

At that time the church was expanding its Bible School outreach by producing video classes. Juan Carlos asked me to set up the system to record and reproduce the classes on CDs which would be sent to churches all over Latin America. To get this going, he and I needed to fly to the USA to bring back the necessary items. His Beechcraft Duke was ideal. We could fly nonstop to Houston, crossing the Gulf of Mexico. Later distribution travels let us explore bits of Peru, Central America, Mexico and USA.

For me, the 'cherry on top of the sundae' was the Beechcraft King Air C 90 Juan Carlos later bought, a turboprop twin, carrying up to 10 passengers. I made many trips in that aircraft. It was by far the most advanced, comfortable, stable aircraft I had ever flown. It had all the the 'bells and whistles' one might ever wish for. It could go high, fast and far. Sadly, a year, later for health reasons, Juan Carlos had to close his business and sell the airplanes. The pastor also sold his airplane. Once again, I was basically grounded.

Not for long. The Church of the Nazarene had moved their offices for Central America and the Caribbean to Guatemala. They flew down a very nice Cessna 210 with retractable landing gear, radar, auto pilot. I was asked to be their pilot. They had rented a nice big hangar with plenty of spare parts. I was back in the air! What a joy it was to serve these dear brothers as we flew all over Central America.

An extremely memorable Nazarene highlight was the planned visit to Guatemala of the General Superintendent (world leader) of their church. An entire year had gone into planning his trip. Now we were flying him to points throughout all of Mexico, starting at the border of Guatemala and ending in Tijuana. My passengers were the General Superintendent, the Mexican Director, the Central American and Caribbean Directors. Together we began 'hedge-hopping' all over Mexico.

That was like a free tour of Mexico for me. But the really exciting saga began when we landed in Tuxtla Gutiérrez, capital of the state of Chiapas. The Governor of Chiapas was an evangelical Christian, very active in the Church of the Nazarene. We were received in his office in the Capital. He presented us with very nice gifts, mine a wood carving of a native Chiapas Indian. We were thankful to have the Governor's interest and blessings on our project, little knowing how much we would need it.

The Nazarenes planned a large service in San Angel Corzo, a rural village in the state of Chiapas, where the Nazarenes had many churches. This meeting would allow an official of the church to prepare new pastors for ordination, as is customary for Nazarenes. We were flying in the General Superintendent to preside. With at least a dozen pastors to be ordained, a great celebration was planned.

But first we needed to get all the attendees to that rural village. When we got to the airport to file a flight plan, the controller informed us that the airfield in San Angel Corzo was closed by order of the military, due to the heavy traffic of drug runners in that area. What a blow to the church--to us all.

The church director of Mexico immediately called for advice from the Governor we had just met in the Capital. He said he would check with the military, to try to obtain special permission. He soon notified us that permission would be impossible, due to many fatal incidents involving drug-runners. BUT the Governor offered us his own helicopter and his pilots! We could fly directly to the village, landing in a soccer field, thus bypassing the 'forbidden' airstrip completely.

So we watched a huge Bell Jet Ranger helicopter land, a 13 passenger plane with two professional pilots. The governor had also thoughtfully packed a cooler full of drinks and snacks. To my glee, as they climbed aboard, the pilots motioned for me to come along on the trip. I took the jump seat between the two pilots, so I could observe their maneuvers for start-up, takeoff and climb-out enroute to the village of San Angel Corzo.

All went well--until the GPS malfunctioned. The shocked pilots had no clue where this village was. They had never flown in the area. Could God have possibly foreknown of this very crisis? Incredibly, a year earlier I had taken the Nazarene directors to that very airstrip. I told the pilots,"Hey, I know how to get there." I saw them exchange dubious looks. How could this gringo possibly know the way, even if he did live in Guatemala?

I insisted that I could get us there. I started by explaining that they should follow this valley until they come to a river that cuts to the right through the mountains. Maybe sensing the confidence in my voice, they hesitatingly responded. Next I told them to cross two valleys, follow another river, go left and fly down that valley to a flat área, turn right and there they'd find the village. Voila! About 45 minutes later we were landing in that very soccer field. The whole town came out to receive us, rejoicing with shouts of praise. We off-loaded the church officials and they headed to the service. I stayed with the pilots. We had a grand time with plenty to eat and drink. Naturally, we had to exchange stories of our flying adventures.

About four in the afternoon, the officials returned. We prepared for the takeoff, engines started with lots of noise and vibrations. But to a fixed-wing pilot like me, things didn't seem right. There was no airstrip, only a huge tree about twenty feet ahead. The captain suddenly made a motion to the co-pilot. I thought he had the same concern about the big tree. The co-pilot loosened his seat belt and got out of the helicopter. Maybe something else was wrong. I was trying to figure out what it might be when the co-pilot opened the passenger door and motioned for me to get out. What had I done? It was hard to hear over the roar of the engine, but he shouted in my ear, "The captain wants you in the front. Take my seat." Whoa! Now I was the copilot! Of a helicopter! The captain yelled, "I will take off, bank left and climb out, then you take it. I will control the power, but you fly it, just like an airplane. Go ahead, take it and try it out." So I did a few banks to the right and left.

Felt good, but I did notice the passengers were very quiet. Hmm, not feeling too confident in my skills? As I approached Tuxtla, by habit I headed for the runway. The captain yelled, "NO! NO! Not the runway! Over there, in front of that building." Well, I could be excused. Compared to 12,000 plus hours flying a my aircraft, I'd only had forty-five minutes with a helicopter—and never landed one before. With the captain's guidance, we did get our passengers on the ground.

Shortly thereafter, Chiqui and I found ourselves once again seeking the Lord's next job. I'd been flying eleven years with the Nazarenes, but now their plane was needed in Africa, so their flying program was gradually phased out. This was yet another 'What next?'

Ah, more of God's marvelous 'advance planning' was revealed. Many years before, a missionary had come to me to share his plans to start a ministry in Guatemala. Jim Zirquel wanted me to fly him around the country searching for some suitable location. After covering most of the middle of the country, he decided that the Lord was leading him to the second largest town in Guatemala, Quetzaltenango. He established Agua Viva Mission (living water) in nearby Xela with plans to develop a Bible school, a church and an aviation program. Aviation would allow them to reach out to outlying areas with extension courses for Christians who could not afford to travel to the school.

So God had a good temporary job for me, flying back and forth from Guatemala City to Jim's Agua Viva location at Xela. While my work for the Nazarenes was decreasing, Jim's plans were progressing and the church was growing. As the flying program grew, he hired the Jacob brothers as pilots. Jim's son was also one of the pilots.

Jim built a hangar, with an apartment for pilots. His planes required a huge hangar. In addition to the single engine Cessna 206, he had--would you believe--a DC-3! That DC-3 was perfect for bringing supplies and groups down from the USA for various community ministries such as medical and construction. The combined Agua Viva ministries were a tremendous outreach, touching many lives.

Then tragedy struck! A tropical storm formed in the Caribbean and was moving inland towards Guatemala. At the same time, a short-term medical team had just arrived from the U.S. to work in the villages near Xela. They were anxious to get started, since their time in Guatemala was limited. Unfortunately, they were all now in Guatemala City, not Xela. And the tropical storm soon became a powerful hurricane.

To land in Xela in hurricane conditions would require an instrument approach which didn't exist. Pilots had long been in discussion with Civil Aeronautics about obtaining approval for an instrument approach to Xela. But establishing one would be very difficult as the only radio contact was a commercial radio station about 3 miles north of the airstrip. So the Civil Aviation Dept. had not approved instrument approach plans.

Now, with severe weather, Jim's mission was refused permission to fly to Xela. On second thought, the airport authorities said they *could* authorize the flight if the mission signed a waiver freeing all parties of any responsibility should something untoward happen. The Agua Viva officials signed the waiver and the mission pilots took off with their medical team.

The weather was indeed terrible flying through the high mountains, with heavy rains, wind and nearly zero visibility. The plane apparently tried once for a landing but failed. They decided to try again. On the second approach, they hit the side of a mountain next to the airstrip. There were no survivors. The mission lost the founder, his son, his son-in-law, the Jacob brother pilots, a doctor and the nurses from the USA. It was the worst tragedy the missionary community had ever suffered.

Jim's wife and remaining family stayed on with Agua Viva, kept the Bible school and church ministries going. They were encouraged to reinstate the aviation program. After three years of much prayer and soul-searching, the decision was made to launch an aviation program. A brand-new Cessna 206, the latest model, was donated to the misión but no pilot was available.

They called me to see if we could work something out. Their plane at mission headquarters was in another town, five hours by car, twenty-four minutes by plane from where I lived. I insisted that, if they wanted me as pilot, the plane had to be based with me in Guatemala City. They agreed to that, plus they gave me the liberty to use the plane for other mission flights.

For about a year I flew for them, as well as for our church. Then a young missionary arrived in Guatemala to begin a teaching ministry. In God's providence, he 'just happened' to be a pilot and instructor. I introduced him to the Agua Viva work in Xela. He was interested and they accepted him as their pilot, relieving me of those duties.

That Agua Viva ministry marked the end of 48 years of flying for me. I did not renew my license, so I can concentrate on preaching, drawing, and teaching.

Today I am also a board member of AGAPE, the mission we started 45 yrs ago. It is still going strong, has one Cessna 206, a great Guatemalan pilot and a good governing board of Guatemalan nationals (plus a gringo, me.) They would love your prayers.

My guiding verse has been 1 Corinthians 9:22. Early on, I keyed in to the last part of the verse, "I have become all things to all people so that *by all possible means* I might save some of them." I interpreted "by all possible means" to include even using an airplane.

As a new missionary putting that interpretation to the test, you can see I discovered that I could use aviation in many different ways to proclaim the Gospel.

Our call came from the Lord. "Woe is me if I do not preach the Gospel." (I Cor 9:16) Preaching, flying, doing biblically based chalk-art talks, the Lord has led me all the way and brought me safely through-- a blessed journey with my precious wife at my side.

As the timeless hymn says, "Through many dangers, toils and snares, we have already come. 'Twas grace that brought us safe thus far and grace will lead us home." (*Amazing Grace* by John Newton, 1779) That will truly be our Final Flight.

WITH GOD, WITH OR WITHOUT WINGS

It's been a life full of adventure, thrills, fascinating people, places and planes. None of it would have been effective without God as my co-pilot. Now my life goes on without airplanes, but definitely not without a sense of purpose and ministry guided by God.

Looking back, I can see His fingerprints all over my life events. I hope you saw it, too. And, hopefully, through these stories from my life, you have caught a glimpse of the many different ways our Lord leads—not just in flying, but relationships, career choices, redirecting mistakes, even in our mundane daily plans.

Maybe while reading, your eyes, your ears, and your heart were opened just a bit more to listen to what He might be saying to you today.

I pray it might be so.

BUSH PILOT IN GOD'S HANDS

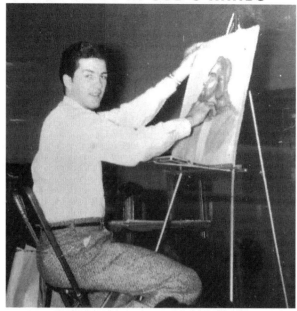

Don Giving chalk-talk 60 yrs ago

60 yrs Later-Still Doing Chalk-Talks

208

Tent Meeting Site for Don & Bud

Bud & Don Donaldson

Brothers and Ministry Partners

On Bahama Mission Seriously Overloaded

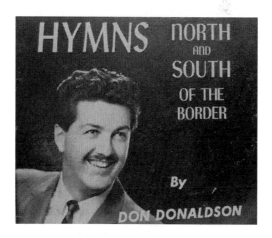

Fund-Raising LP for Plane

Life Changing Crash

Have Kombi Will Travel

Chiqui-Charming Senorita

First Guatemala TV Programs

Loading Supplies for Missionaries

Happy, Handsome Family

Soldiers Check Passengers in Guerilla Area

Safe Flying in Amazing Amazon

Painting cheer onto walls of

Shell-Mera Hospital in Ecuador

Street Evangelism in Guatemala

Pilot to Tower

Careful Concentration Calculating Fuel

Preaching Jesus' Love for the Whole World

Happy Family through the Years

Wordless Witness Tract